caddie sense

caddie sense

REVELATIONS OF A PGA
TOUR CADDIE ON PLAYING
THE GAME OF GOLF

Michael Carrick and Steve Duno

THOMAS DUNNE BOOKS
st. martin's press ✹ new york

THOMAS DUNNE BOOKS.
An imprint of St. Martin's Press.

Interior photographs by Andrea Liptac

Design by Lisa Pifher

www.stmartins.com

Library of Congress Cataloging-in-Publication Data

Carrick, Michael.
    Caddie sense : revelations of a PGA Tour caddie on playing the game of golf/Michael Carrick and Steve Duno ; foreword by Tom Kite.—1st ed.
        p. cm.
    ISBN 0-312-20286-5
    1. Caddying.   2. Caddies.   3. PGA Tour (Association) 4. Kite, Tom.   5. Carrick, Michael.   I. Duno, Steve.   II. Title.
GV977.C27 2000
796.352—dc21   00-027276

First Edition: May 2000

10 9 8 7 6 5 4 3 2 1

contents

foreword

by
Tom Kite

Throughout the years there have been numerous books written about the PGA Tour, and about the lifestyle that goes along with being a member of that organization. Most of these books have either taken the point of view of the golfers or of those in the media writing about the players. While both perspectives are interesting, the most accurate (if not the most colorful) view would be that of a caddie.

The caddie is a unique member of our traveling circus. He never gets the opportunity to hit a golf shot in any tournament. And yet he is critically important to the outcome of that event.

In my case, I would never want Mike to actually hit a shot for me. As a matter of fact, when Mike and I have played golf together, I am always amazed at how a caddie who knows so much about the game could be so inept at playing. Now, he is not the worst player I have seen, by any means. Most times he gets around the course somewhere in the 80s. But when one hangs around the greatest golfers in the world on a daily basis, and has access to their knowledge and expertise, it seems reasonable that some of it should rub off. Such is not the case with Mike, or for most caddies on Tour, for that matter.

Mike Carrick is not on my bag because of his talent at playing the game. He is on my bag because he is a good friend. We did not know each other before I went on Tour, but after nearly twenty years of working for me, he has become a trusted friend and companion. Some weeks I will actually spend more time with Mike than I do with my wife and kids. And while that is not necessarily the way either of us would like it to be, that is the way it is when you are trying to make a living playing golf.

We have to be able to get along under all sorts of circumstances. If any of my attention gets directed toward Mike, wondering if he is doing his job correctly, then it takes my focus away from trying to play the upcoming shot. Many times a brief loss of concentration can cost thousands of dollars. I trust Mike to do his job, just as he trusts me to do mine. And I can assure you, there are few in the caddie business as competent and qualified as Mike.

Obviously there are other talents required of caddies. The first would probably be timeliness. It is impossible for a caddie to do his job if he is not there. Since Mike started working for me in the early '80s, he has only been late one time, at the 1980 British Open, the very first week he started working for me. Now, he wasn't really late for the tee time. But I was almost finished warming up when he strolled onto the practice range. That was not a good way to start a relationship. He was being paid to carry the bag; that included getting them to the range. He would be upset if I did not try my best every day; I just expected the same out of him. From that moment on, there would be no excuse for being late, for either of us. To both our credit, there never has been.

Another important characteristic I look for in a caddie is consistency. When we are coming down the closing holes in a tournament trying for a win, my nerves jumping like crazy, the last person I want on my bag is someone more nervous than me. I need a voice of reason and calmness, regardless of what I am feeling inside. Neither do I want with me a caddie who is down in the mouth and dragging 20 yards behind after I have just made a couple of bogies. My caddie needs to appear excited to be there despite the day's score.

And, of course, there are the usual job requirements that everyone knows about: getting the yardage, knowing where the pins are located, cleaning the clubs and balls, helping with club selection, and reading the putts are but a few of them.

But by far the most important characteristic I look for in a caddie is a good sense of humor. There are so many wonderful stories that happen every day on the course. As with life, these are best shared with friends. The ability to laugh in the face of a difficult situation can help put it into its proper perspective. And in so many cases, just being able to smile at a bad lie or an unfortunate break can make the next shot a whole lot easier. Mike and I have cried together over the tournaments that got away, but we have shared many more laughs than tears. That is why we are still together.

Caddie Sense will, no doubt, bring you into our world. Hopefully you will enjoy the book as much as we have enjoyed the ride.

introduction

Of the countless golf books written and purchased over the years, most have been authored by renowned professional players. This makes perfect sense; who better to teach the public how to swing a golf club than the world's best? Thousands of aficionados have learned invaluable lessons from the legendary likes of Hogan, Palmer, Nicklaus, Faldo, Norman, and many others (including a young upstart named Woods). These champions have all been able to share with the public their secrets for success, from basic swing fundamentals right down to mastering specialized trouble shots.

Though entertaining and effective, these books have provided the avid student of golf with only one perspective on the game—that of the pro player. In the search for mastery of any avocation, exposure to differing points of view has always been one of the keys to true understanding and improvement. To that end, why not provide the reader with a prescriptive book on golf as seen from a slightly different, perhaps fresher, perspective?

Caddie Sense does just that. Written from the perspective of a veteran PGA Tour caddie, it makes available to the average golfer, for the first time, intimate playing strategies used by the best of the best. As president of the Professional Tour Caddies Association and caddie to the legendary Tom Kite for over seventeen years, I am able to provide you, the reader, with rare, inside-the-ropes glimpses of the game and relate just what it takes to play and win on a championship-caliber level. This book will take you on a trip past the barrier ropes and up close to the real action; actual conversations between players and their caddies are revealed and discussed, with a focus on the winning strategies used during tournament play.

Over the last seventeen years, I've had the great honor of being there next to Tom Kite on his way to becoming one of the most successful players in PGA Tour history. Those years have taught me things about the game that just don't come across on television or in magazines. This book will share much of that insider knowledge with you, while at the same time revealing entertaining details about the professional and personal lives of the PGA Tour players and their colorful caddies, untapped fountainheads of golfing lore and know-how.

Caddie Sense is the very first strategic book on golf written by a Tour caddie. Most golf books, written by players, have focused primarily on the mechanics of the golf swing and much less on basic and advanced game strategy. Player-generated books typically have focused on fundamentals such as curing a hook or slice, how to grip the club, how to set up to the ball, or how to hit from difficult lies. This book takes a slightly different approach by focusing more on proven course management strategies than on technical aspects of the swing. You will enjoy a more complete overview of the subtleties of the game and, for the first time, receive inside information that will help you plot out effective winning "campaigns" for the rounds ahead, in much the same fashion that the pros do.

Caddie Sense focuses more on showing readers how to plan a round of golf (and how to respond to and take advantage of a given set of circumstances on the course) than on how to properly swing a driver or 5-iron. A caddie helps a player to excel with the cards he or she has been dealt; this advisory capacity of the caddie is in fact the heart and soul of the book and what gives it its unique market niche. Think of this book as if it were *your own personal caddie.*

This is not to suggest that *Caddie Sense* would not be helpful to beginners. As a primer on the vital fundamentals of strategy, it takes a back seat to no book. It will provide beginners and more advanced golfers with a clear sense of the fundamental positions and techniques needed to insure consistent results from tee to green. This book provides the essentials, while also teaching how to deal with the almost endless variables that can present themselves during a round of golf. This versatility makes the book useful to all levels of players. Intermediate and advanced golfers, who by and large ignore the plethora of beginner instructional golf books now crowding the shelves, will find *Caddie Sense* to be a refreshing, invaluable read. Above all, this book opens up an exclusive window onto the world of professional golf, allowing you to be privy to on-course dramas not often revealed to the public.

Part One, entitled "A Caddie's Life: The Sporting World's Most Unique Occupation," defines for the reader the nuts and bolts of the caddying profession, touching on topics such as origins of the trade, how to become a caddie, how caddies and players team up, life on the road, what caddies get paid, and how they learn their trade. Throughout this section, I'll touch on the unique flavor of the job and introduce you to the various characters I have met who have helped to create one of the most unusual, offbeat, and demanding ways to make a living.

Part Two, entitled "The Caddie/Player Relationship," reveals the complex relations that go on between caddies and players. Types of contractual agreements are revealed, as are the intricate and often fragile workings of the partnership. Different players bring with them differing expectations of what a caddie's job should be, some wanting very little decisive input, others wanting a great deal. Many players choose a caddie for his or her "cheerleading" abilities, while others simply want a quiet, capable club carrier. Part Two also touches on the emotional conflicts that can and do occur between caddie and player, which can often result in a "divorce." A window into the psyche of the sport, this section will illuminate behind-the-scenes emotional dramas rarely seen by the public on tournament day.

Part Three, entitled "Playing the Game," is the focal point of the book, providing the reader with tournament-proven strategic tips on all aspects of the game, as seen from the professional Tour caddie's point of view. Second in importance only to the player's inherent skills, the tutelage of a seasoned PGA Tour caddie has been and continues to be an integral part of the winning formula for pro golfers the world over. Throughout this section, I will make you privy to many actual situations that Tom and I have encountered during our years of competition, in hopes that they might entertain and enlighten. Strategic advice shared with you in this part of the book include

- Equipment basics: tools of the trade that can make a difference
- Knowing your course and becoming familiar with each hole
- Basic set-up positions used by the pros
- The decision-making process: how to choose a club and play a shot
- Special shots
- Putting strategies
- Common mistakes made by amateurs
- The rigors of competition
- How the pros prepare, practice, and stay fit

The epilogue will summarize just what it has felt like for me to have been part of such a winning tradition, with such a great champion as Tom Kite. In addition, I'll take this space to talk about the future of the Tour, its players, and its caddies. The importance of reestablishing youth involvement in caddie programs is a pet project of mine and will be discussed here as well.

I hope that the information offered in the following pages of *Caddie Sense* helps to improve your game by getting you to think in a more strategic manner, plotting out your moves in advance rather than plodding through moment to moment. I also hope that you enjoy the window that I have attempted to open up for you, a window with a private view onto one of the world's oldest and most beloved games, the game we all treasure—golf.

PART ONE

A Caddie's Life: The Sporting
World's Most Unique Occupation

Pebble

The 1992 U.S. Open began damp and foggy, with no wind at all. Scores would be low, and too many players would be left in the hunt. Both Tom and I wanted that to change; we wanted the Pacific sea breezes to blow hard, to weed out the field and give us our chance. Tom was one of the game's greatest wind players; as the offshore gusts increased in strength, so would his confidence. We would have to wait until the last round to get our wish.

When Sunday morning came, we were only one shot back. As I got ready for our last round, I wondered if this would finally be our day, or just another one of many major disappointments. The week had gone well for us up to that point; Tom had been unusually relaxed and confident and hadn't even played a practice round on Monday, instead opting to show up in mid-afternoon to hit a few balls and to work on his short game. He knew the course well and wouldn't need to put in quite as much practice time because of it. Tom had spent the previous week with his family in Baltimore, going to a few baseball games, playing some fun rounds, and having a good time with his kids and wife. He was relaxed, almost serene.

I was lucky enough to be able to stay with some friends in a neighborhood called Spanish Bay, close to Pebble. Having a posh place to stay in such beautiful surroundings really put me at ease. Both Tom and I went into the week feeling confident and ready.

During a practice round on Wednesday, we got an inkling of things to come. On the par-3 12th hole, Tom hit a pure shot that bounced three times and then dove right into the hole. We laughed and "high-fived" each other; the feeling of sudden confidence and optimism that a hole-in-one brings was just how Tom was feeling about his game all that week. Everything seemed to be coming together in just the right way; we felt the surge of a big, well-timed wave carrying us, a feeling every winning PGA player and caddie knows and remembers, always.

I had never seen Tom so focused and calm. A few weeks earlier, he'd finished in eighth place at Jack's Memorial Tournament, overcoming some early missed putts to finish strong. Throughout that tournament, though, he'd seemed relaxed and thoughtful. On the last hole he came up to me and said, "Mike, if we stay this patient, then we've got a chance at Pebble."

The "one shot at a time" maxim, easy to say and hard to do, really was happening for him the week at Pebble. It was a beautiful thing to see. Bogey or birdie meant nothing to him; he just went about his business, one shot at a time, to the very end.

The course started out easy that Thursday. With no wind, Pebble was giving up some low scores. By Saturday, Gil Morgan had become the first player to get to double figures under par in U.S. Open history, reaching 12 under through seven holes that day. His fantastic score wouldn't last, though, for Pebble finally began to bare her teeth by the end of the third round. After a triple-bogey on the 8th hole, Gil lost his confidence, and the lead.

I don't think I have ever seen a more sudden and brutal change of conditions anywhere. The wind began to howl that Sunday, stronger than I'd seen even during any of the British Opens I'd worked. Both Tom and I were elated. We knew Mother Nature had just cut the field in half. "This is it, Mike," he'd said, smiling and hungry.

As the wind howled in off the Pacific, the greens got harder and faster. Club selection became an almost surreal experience; many players and their caddies weren't on speaking terms by the end of that day.

But Tom and I knew each other too well. I could club him in the howling winds of Pebble, the rarified mountain air of Colorado, or the humid heat of Houston. Put us on the moon and I could pull the right club for Tom. When the wind blows like it did that Sunday, any player without an experienced caddie didn't stand a chance.

Tom had shot a steady 2 under par on Saturday to get us to 3 under for the tournament. We began the last round one back, in the second to last group, with Mark Brooks. Then came the winds.

All week Tom's ball striking hadn't been superb, but his concentration, focus, and putting had all been stellar. He birdied the 1st hole with a great second shot to inside of six feet, but he didn't birdie the reachable par-5 2nd. He parred the 3rd after having to hit a 150-yard, 4-iron approach shot into the teeth of the Pacific maelstrom and negotiating a tricky downhill, downwind putt to within tap-in range. His drive on the 4th was right down the middle, but his second shot got caught by the wind and ended up in the back bunker. The pin was in the back of the green, and his bunker shot would be downwind. With the greens firmed up, Tom knew he was dead in the water, with little chance to get up and down. After hitting a great shot, the ball ended up forty feet below the hole. Tom laughed and joked, "I hit a pure bunker shot, and I'm still forty feet away!" It was how he said it that shocked me; there was not a lick of anger in him. He was *laughing* and having a good old time. That's when I knew he was in the proper mindset to win. He three-putted to make double-bogey, and forgot all about it before arriving at the 5th tee.

The 5th was an uphill par-3. Tom pushed his shot into the front bunker, blasted out twelve feet left of the hole, courting bogie or worse. Instead, he knocked the left-to-right swinging putt into the center of the hole for a great par. He then birdied the 6th with a great knockdown 6-iron into the gale, followed by a long putt. Then we came to the short 7th, normally a wedge shot. Playing into a fierce right-to-left wind that day, the hole required that Tom hit a 6-iron. His tee shot was blown left of the green, into a questionable lie. Tom calmly put his lob wedge to the ball, lofting it up high and setting it down nicely onto the hard green. The ball bounced, rolled, and then, amazingly, hit the pin and dropped in for a birdie. The shot instantly reminded me of Watson's great chip-in against Nicklaus. When I saw it go in, I got the winning chills; maybe this was our time. But there was still too much work ahead, so I put it out of my mind.

The par-4 8th had a blind, uphill tee shot, with the fairway dropping off two hundred fifty yards out; the best shot would stop short of it, on level grass. Normally a 3-wood tee shot, the wind was gusting above 40 mph. Clubbing him was no easy matter; Tom thought 3-iron, but I felt it was a perfect 4-iron. Normally you go with the player's feel, but I was firmly convinced of it being a 4-iron. Tom knew I rarely disagreed unless I was dead sure, so he went with the 4-iron. Though I was unable to see it from the tee box, the shot landed eight yards short of the drop-off, right in the middle of the fairway. Upon approaching the ball, I could breathe again. I still had a job. Tom parred the hole and gave me a big old "thank you" smile.

On the 9th, Tom pushed his approach shot right of the green, toward the beach. After finding it in the heavy rough, he made good contact, amazingly got it onto the green, and ended up two-putting for a bogey. A nice bogey, considering the circumstances. In the U.S. Open, bogey is not always bad; on the contrary, it is often welcome, particularly when the greens are undulating and fast as a hardwood floor.

Going into the 10th hole, we still had a two-shot lead over Jeff Sluman. Tom put his tee shot into a fairway bunker and had no chance to make the green due to the wind. He played his next shot short of the green by about fifty yards, then got up and down from there for a great par. Tom is deadly with his 60-degree wedge, and he proved it on that crucial hole.

He went on to par the 11th, birdie the 12th with a brilliant thirty-footer, and par the 13th. Then came the 14th hole, a long par-5 that Tom hadn't been able to reach in two all week. On Sunday, though, the wind was howling straight toward the green. Tom wanted driver, and I was all for it. The drive was perfect, leaving him with a 3-wood to the green, if he wanted to chance it. The green on the 14th was extremely slick, however; even players laying up weren't able to hold the green that day. "How about an easy 3-wood right into the front bunker?" he asked me. I instantly knew that this was the perfect solution. Tom was an expert bunker player and could cozy the ball up to the pin from a greenside trap much more easily than from one hundred yards out. "Go for it" was all I said, watching him pull the club out. The ball ended up in the rough just short of the bunker; from there, he made a great pitch with the 60-degree wedge to within four feet of the pin. Tom buried the putt for birdie, one of the few at the 14th that day. A truly amazing display of course management. We were ahead by four shots, and we could both taste it. But would it be enough?

A 3-wood on the 15th found the left rough. All Tom could do was hack it out just short of the green, from where he pitched in close and made par. Tom's 3-wood tee shot at the 16th just drifted into the right rough; I didn't think he could get it to the green, but the ball came out nicely, landed on the front edge, and rolled all the way to the rear fringe. He chipped to inside of four feet but missed the putt. As he muttered to himself, we headed for the brutal par-3 17th, 235 yards, right into the gale.

We both knew that 3-wood wasn't enough, but the idea of hitting driver (with the Pacific right behind the green) wasn't very appealing either. We decided to put a 3-wood into the front bunker, in hopes that Tom's short game would come through for us again. Drawing an awkward lie on the left side of the trap, Tom hit a brilliant shot to within six feet of the pin, but missed his par with a pure, slow-rolling putt that nearly dropped in. Still ahead by two shots, we were both very calm. Tom was playing solid golf under the worst wind conditions we'd ever seen. He was rock-steady, almost peaceful.

The par-5 18th at Pebble—tough at best, a nightmare at worst. We needed a bogey or better to win the U.S. Open. The hole had called for a 3-wood tee shot all week, due to the narrow fairway landing area. In order to make par, the tee shot had to end up on the short stuff, so nearly everyone had been leaving the big stick in the bag. Upon reaching the tee box, Tom casually asked, "What do think about driver here, Mike?" The conditions screamed 3-wood, but he was so confident and at ease that I just said, "Yep, that's the club. Put a good swing on it." On the outside I was confident and sure; inside I was quaking over the thought of him hitting driver. But that is the essence of the caddie/player relationship—go with what the player is most confident with and support the decision. Tom knew driver was the club, and did not hesitate to ask for it. Sometimes you can't go by the numbers; you need to go with the feeling in your player's head, hands, and heart.

As soon as he hit it, Tom turned to me and said, "Best swing of the week." He didn't even watch it, not for a moment. I did, though, all the way, like a hungry hawk. The ball landed smack in the middle of the fairway, in perfect position. We walked down the fairway, still not thinking about a win until the next shot, which would be a 5-iron lay-up. Tom pured it, leaving a perfect wedge to the green. When his ball finally rapped down onto the firm putting surface and stopped fifteen feet from the pin, I suddenly came out of my trance and knew that, barring any sad miracles, we had just won the U.S. Open. I watched Tom, still wearing his game face, calmly two-putt us to a treasured victory, the most memorable and meaningful of our lives. All of our experiences, all of our skills, victories, and defeats, came together that day in perfect synchronicity to give us what we'd wanted for so long. We'd worked together as a team as well as any pairing could have and won the U.S. Open, arguably the hardest of the four majors. And don't think for a second that the player is the only one to celebrate or to boast. The caddie of a major winner feels the swell of pride just as strongly, every time. I know I did that day.

Heritage

Golf, though ever-changing, remains steadfastly within its traditions. One of those many traditions still honored today is that of the caddie, whose place in the annals of the old game remains, at least on a professional level, alive and well. Once viewed as rakish, poverty-stricken outcasts, today's caddies, when at the top of their professions, write books, star in national television commercials, and become celebrities in their own right. Quite a change from the days when the average bag handler was considered a bawdy, hard-drinking, antisocial rogue, paid just enough to keep him walking the fairways and tipping his tankard.

To give a sense of perspective on the longevity of the game and its traditions, consider that royal enthusiasts such as Mary Queen of Scots and King James II were playing golf back in the sixteenth and seventeenth centuries, and that the "Old Course" at St. Andrews in Scotland has been in operation since the seventeenth century. Moneyed gentlemen playing the game would hire down-and-out day laborers to carry their clubs for them; these "cawdys" (a name used to describe itinerant water carriers and messengers in eighteenth-century Scotland) became the prototype for today's "caddies."

Until the late nineteenth century, golfers were by and large considered to be amateurs. The professional golfer was still virtually a fictional character (barring those few rapscallions who made a living gambling on the game). When professional tournaments were first organized and played, golfers taking on a professional status were looked down upon by the more wealthy, privileged amateur class, who felt that the practice of playing golf for money cheapened the game. In truth, those who chose to turn professional were often from a less "elegant" class, skilled working-class players who wanted to turn their skills into money. In fact, many of the early professionals started out as caddies or groundskeepers, men with intimate knowledge of the courses, conditions, and strategies. These working-class individuals had been servicing the privileged classes for so long that when they decided to actually play the game (and excel at it), their old bosses thought it the height of bad taste.

The onset of professional tournaments (and the money generated by them) did more to better the financial lot of caddies than perhaps any other development. Previously, club caddies would report for work in the early morning and hope to get assigned to a gentleman player, who, if feeling generous, would pay and tip the caddie enough to justify the effort. Few club caddies ever made a good enough living to substantially change their lives for the better. Life for these men became a day-to-day struggle, with no discernable future ahead of them.

The onset of professionalism in golf did two things for the caddie. It provided those skilled at the game with a new outlet for making a decent living. Legendary nineteenth-century Scottish players such as old Tom Morris, Tom Kidd (winner of the first British Open), Bob Martin, and Jamie Anderson, all starting out as caddies at St. Andrews, went on to fame and financial comfort. Also, a caddie lucky enough to team up with a successful professional could make substantially more money than a club caddie, who (in the nineteenth century) might be paid only a shilling per round. Though many elitists mourned the coming of the professional golfer, caddies by and large were not among them.

By the early twentieth century, golf had become as popular a sport in the United States as it already was in Europe. Still largely a sport of the economically privileged, each country club established a caddie pool, modeled after the European system. A caddie master managed the assigning of caddies to players and also saw to financial and disciplinary matters. In addition to adults, adolescents as young as twelve found caddying to be an effective way of earning money while still being outside in the fresh air, close to the game.

The country club caddie continues to maintain one distinct advantage over the Tour caddie; he or she need not learn the player's game, apart from knowing his or her handicap, or knowing how far he or she can hit a driver, 7-iron, or wedge. A country club caddie switches from player to player and need not key in on the player's temperament or capabilities. The only imperative is to know the course well enough to recommend the proper club and shot and to be congenial enough to rake in the tips.

Club caddies became an institution and far outnumbered those working for professional golfers. Until the mid-twentieth century, they were an ingrained institution.

Everything changed with the invention of the motorized golf cart, which became not only a welcome convenience to thousands of weekend golfers not wanting to walk three to four miles of fairway but also a great money-maker for golf courses. Adding fifteen, twenty, or twenty-five dollars to the price of a round helped increase profits immensely; most clubs were happy to invest in these strange little "go-carts." Originally, it was even thought that they would speed up play, but, oddly enough, the opposite has happened.

Within a short span of time, these electric or gas-powered gadgets began to change caddying forever. Maintaining a large staff of caddies was no longer necessary; the fee (and the tips) charged to players for a caddie's services now all went into the club's coffers. With the exception of a few exclusive facilities, club caddies virtually became an extinct animal in the United States and in much of the world.

The remaining sanctuary for the caddie remains, of course, the professional golf tours. Players on the PGA, LPGA, Senior, Nike, European, and Asian Tours, as well as on the various mini-tours throughout the world, all still use the same time-honored skills of the caddie, not merely out of respect for the tradition but for the competitive edge having one provides.

Just a passing thought: Ben Hogan, Byron Nelson, Lee Trevino, and Chi Chi Rodriguez all started out as caddies.

What Caddies Do

A PGA Tour caddie has one of the most unique jobs in all of professional sports. To the uninitiated, he or she might seem only to be responsible for toting some forty-odd pounds of golfing equipment over a rolling, seven-thousand-yard course, fixing divots, and cleaning a club off after the shot has been made. In fact, the job of a PGA Tour caddie involves much more than this oversimplified, "Sherpa-like" image might suggest. In addition to carrying the equipment, a caddie must do the following:

- Maintain the equipment
- Determine and calculate accurate yardages to various key points on the golf course
- Have a detailed understanding of the course layout and architecture
- Know from which direction the prevailing winds are most likely to blow
- Understand the basic golf strategies most suited to the player and the course
- Be familiar with the unique characteristics of each green, including pin placement, grain, slope, speed rating, and current overall level of preparation
- Be intimately familiar with the player's strengths and weaknesses
- Give reliable advice on club selection and shot execution
- Be emotionally supportive during times of competitive pressure
- Be able to inspire confidence

- Expect that even the most magnanimous player will sometimes lose his or her cool
- Keep track of a player's score
- Be positive at all times
- Know the rules

A PGA Tour caddie, in other words, must be counselor, coach, politician, statistician, meteorologist, golfer, craftsman, cheerleader, scapegoat, landscape architect, and friend, all wrapped up into an enduring walking machine. Denied of such an aide, Tour professionals would be at a serious disadvantage. In fact, professional golf as we know it would just not be the same game.

In no other sport can one find the same unique bond between two persons. Though two-player sports do exist (as in doubles tennis, beach volleyball, bobsledding, or figure skating), in golf, the caddie is not a player *per se*, but rather an assistant, allowed to be right in the thick of things. Oddly, the only other competitive relationships that come close are race car drivers and their pit crews, or perhaps even jockeys and their horses, in which the rider helps with direction and decision-making while the horse does all the actual work. And no, I am not equating professional golfers to horses, even though they are both thoroughbreds!

On Becoming a Caddie

My own story is typical of how someone usually gets started caddying. I began caddying in 1958 when I was twelve years old, at the Riverside Country Club in New Brunswick, Canada. A beautiful, old, medium-length Donald Ross course, Riverside was tight through the trees, with small, fast greens. Youngsters like myself were the mainstay of the caddie pool, mainly because we were willing to carry a member's clubs for seventy-five cents per round. The perk that kept me working there each summer was that all caddies got to play the course for free every weekday morning until eight A.M., at which point the members would begin to arrive in force. My buddies and I would ride bikes four miles to the club at sunrise, each carrying three or four clubs, and play our hearts out, then go down to the caddie shack and put our names on the list. I can't think of a better way for a kid to learn the game than to play one round, then caddie a second. Knowing what I do now about the sleeping habits of teenagers on vacation, I'm amazed at my eagerness back then to get up at five A.M. each day, just to go walk seven or eight miles beside a sleepy, grumpy, bad-tipping 30-handicapper.

I'd quickly gotten hooked on the space and on the daily dose of nature. The course was a quiet sanctuary for me, filled with trees, rolling grass, lakes, birds, and other wildlife. To me, it was like going hiking every day, and getting to mix a great game in with it at the same time. Being a shy and introverted only child, I found golf to be the ideal sport, as it was much more self-reliant than team sports such as baseball, football, or basketball. Though I liked other sports, I quickly developed a special love for the links, one that has lasted for over forty years.

Though a decent player, I've never been good enough to make a living at it. I knew that way back in my teens, but in my heart I still wanted to someday find a way to become involved in golf at a higher level. Setting that dream aside temporarily, I enrolled at the University of New Brunswick in the late sixties and got a degree in physical education. During the summers I continued caddying and, in 1968, finally got the chance to work a series of small pro tournaments in the area.

Jay Dolan, a club pro from Lester, Massachusetts, was the first really good player I ever caddied for. He and his dad owned a small twelve-hole course in Lester, nine holes on one side of the road and three on the other. I think it's still the only twelve-hole course I've ever seen. The locals loved it, because it allowed them to play a round in under three hours. I was assigned to Jay at one of the tournaments; we got along right off and did well enough together for him to ask me to carry his bag on the local circuit that fall. I immediately said yes, and started down a road that, with few detours, I'm still on.

I caddied for Jay for a few years on the local circuit. Then, upon completing college, I taught school for a year, but couldn't resist the urge to travel. In the fall of 1971, Jay asked me to join him on the Tour, as a way to see the country. I readily agreed, not knowing what was in store for me. The first tournament I worked with Jay that fall was the club pro tournament, that year held at Pinehurst Country Club in Pinehurst, North

Carolina, arguably one of the finest and most prestigious courses in the world. Not a bad place to start a career! Though he didn't finish in the money, it was an experience I still think back on from time to time. Pinehurst was expertly manicured and reeked of tradition and professionalism, more so than any course I'd ever seen. The pomp and the caliber of play drew me into the game as never before.

After working Pinehurst with Jay, I took some time off and hitchhiked down to Miami to see my uncle, who'd been living there for some time. While there, I saw an ad in a local paper calling for experienced caddies to work what was then called the "World Cup," being played in Palm Beach Gardens. I applied and, on the strength of my experience with Jay Dolan, was accepted into the caddie pool. I was matched with Don Gammon, a player from Rhodesia. Though we did not finish in the money, the experience and exposure was invaluable to me, as I befriended a number of players and caddies who would eventually influence the direction of my career.

After the World Cup, I took a chance and hitched a ride north with two colorful caddies named Whitey and Chief to Wilmington, Delaware, the site of that year's Azalea Tournament. I rejoined Jay there, but he continued to struggle, missing the cut. We then traveled together to Hilton Head, South Carolina, in an attempt to qualify for the Heritage Tournament at Harbour Town Golf Links (to this day my favorite Tour course). Back then, for those who did not make it through Monday qualifying, a satellite tournament was usually available at a nearby course, which offered a small purse. In fact, Tom's very first win came at one of these events, aptly named the "Hope of Tomorrow," in Palm Springs. Unfortunately, that week found Jay and I competing in that "consolation" tournament instead of the real deal.

Next it was on to Orlando to qualify for the Disney Tournament. Jay once again failed to get in, and decided it was time to go home. I stuck around and managed to get work with a fellow Canadian by the name of Wiff Hommenich. He failed to make the cut, so I headed back to my uncle's place in Miami.

The last tournament of that year was the Bahamas Open. Capable caddies were in short supply, so tournament officials arranged free boat transportation for anyone willing to go. I was very willing, and found myself steaming out of Miami, en route to the islands. As far as I was concerned, it didn't get any better. I worked with several players, and had the time of my life.

Upon returning to Miami from the Bahamas, I spent the holidays with my uncle, and actually played golf on Christmas Day, a real treat for a Canadian. The first tournament of 1972 was the Los Angeles Open, however, and I was 3,000 miles away in Miami, with two hundred dollars to my name. So, on New Year's Eve, I started hitchhiking to California, needing to be in L.A. in three days.

I made it to Houston in two; the people I'd gotten a ride from were kind enough to take me to the airport, where I boarded a cheap night flight to Los Angeles, using most of the cash I had left. Upon arriving, I hitchhiked to the Rancho Park golf course, site of that year's Los Angeles Open. After getting a ticket for hitchhiking on the freeway, I finally made it to the course, and, as luck would have it, ran into a fellow named Shayne Grier, an experienced Tour caddie who would eventually become my mentor on Tour. He and another caddie named Andy Dollar let me stay with them at their place by the beach. When Andy called in sick that week, I filled in for him at the L.A. Open. I was finally on Tour.

After the L.A. Open, I continued traveling with my new adopted family, a gypsy caravan of caddies. After a few weeks of hopping from bag to bag, Shayne introduced me to Dave Eichelberger, a Tour player of considerable skills. He needed a steady caddie, and I readily volunteered for the job. We jelled perfectly, and decided to give it a go. I caddied for Dave for nearly three years, and for the first time learned the intricacies of caddying for one player instead of a new golfer each week. Working with Dave every week allowed me to become familiar with his strengths and weaknesses, which in turn helped me assist him in choosing the right club and type of shot for each situation on the course. By far, my experience with Dave helped make me into an effective Tour caddie.

That was it—I was hooked. Despite having a teaching degree, I decided to devote myself to gallivanting all over the world with a bunch of good-natured scoundrels, learning the ropes and making some money in the process. And I found a profitable way to stay close to the game I loved.

After working with Dave, I carried for Leonard Thompson for a short time, then moved on to Steve Melnyk for three years or so. A great guy, Steve had had an exceptional amateur record. Playing for the University of Florida, he'd won both the U.S. *and* the British Amateurs, one of only a handful of golfers to ever do so. Strangely, Steve didn't turn pro right away; after winning the U.S. Amateur (back when it was still stroke play and not the current match play format), he decided that the Tour life wasn't for him. Instead, he went into the insurance business for a few years, only playing "customer" golf during that time. Then, after seeing that some of the players he'd once beaten handily were now making good money on the Tour, Steve decided to give it a go and got through the qualifying school on his first try. He played for eight or nine years with some success but never did win a tournament. Toward the end, he had the misfortune to slip on a cart path in Phoenix, fracturing his elbow in the process. While sitting out the injury, he became involved for the first time in broadcasting and took to it well. The combination of a smooth voice and a keen golfing mind made him a welcome commodity in the booth or on the course, microphone in hand. Steve now has part ownership of a golf development firm in the Jacksonville area that builds courses and renovates old ones. Intelligent and sharp, Steve is a friend whom I enjoyed working for immensely and who helped hone my caddying skills to their sharpest.

Leaving Steve was a tough decision for me, as he had become a great friend. He had cut back on his schedule, though, and wasn't playing well. He suggested I look for another bag, so I teamed up with Victor Regalado, a Mexican player with streaky luck. He was eligible for the Tournament of Champions that year, which took us to sunny San Diego, at the La Costa

Resort and Spa. A great memory from that week for me was playing a practice round with Lee Trevino, one of the best ball strikers I'd ever seen. That week I think he had missed two fairways, total, and went on to win the tournament.

I finished out the year with Victor, who had managed to make three top tens in a row. Toward the end of the year, the caddie for Lon Hinkle informed me that he would be retiring and could set me up with Lon if I wanted. I jumped at the chance, as Lon was a great player who had won the Bing Crosby Tournament (now the AT&T) and also the World Series of Golf. Lon had length and a decent short game but was an inconsistent putter, ultimately the telling factor during the 1980 U.S. Open, won by Nicklaus. Tee to green, Lon played as well or better than Jack that week, but he didn't sink crucial putts. Constantly missing five- to ten-footers, he ended up in third place behind Nicklaus and Asao Aoki, both of whom sunk putts when it counted. Though still a great payday for us both, it was in the end a frustrating experience.

My introduction to Tom Kite came back in 1978, while I was still working for Steve Melnyck. Steve hadn't qualified for the British Open that year and wasn't entitled to an exemption, leaving me free to pick up someone else's bag that week. The Open was at St. Andrews that year; as I'd never been to golf's homeland before, I was determined to find someone in need of a caddie with experience. After checking around, I learned that Tom Kite's regular caddie, Dennis "Disco" Turning, chose not to travel overseas, leaving Tom without a caddie. After a brief talk, he hired me on for the tournament, provided I'd pay my lodging and travel expenses. I jumped at the chance, not only for the opportunity to walk the fairways of St. Andrews but also for the chance to carry for one of the world's best golfers.

I flew over with Shayne Grier, then the caddie to Hubert Green. Shayne, more than anyone else, had taught me how to find a bag, where to stay, how to travel cheaply, and how to please the player. At the time, the airlines had inexpensive standby fares to Europe; unfortunately you often had to wait hours and sometimes days to get on a plane. Shayne and I waited standby at JFK airport in New York City and ended up missing a flight by just two places in line. Then, after being told that the next standby list wouldn't be compiled for a few hours, we left the airport to get some dinner. Upon returning, we discovered that a list had already been started, and we were now on the bottom of it. Just as I began envisioning Tom Kite (who'd already flown over) walking down the first fairway carrying his own bag and planning my demise, we squeezed onto a plane bound for Edinburgh.

As Shayne and I weren't exactly rich men back then (or now, for that matter), we couldn't afford to rent or hire a car to get us over to St. Andrews from the airport. So, with no other options, we stuck out our thumbs and hitched to the world's most famous golf course, each carrying one suitcase and a whole lot of enthusiasm.

Almost immediately, a gaunt, happy young fellow in an old MGB GT four-seater stopped for us and agreed to take us to St. Andrews, as he was on his way there as well. Sitting in the left front passenger's seat (a shock to most Americans), I buckled in and proceeded to barely survive a 90-mph ride down twisty, narrow country roads. Such was my introduction to Scotland, the mother of all caddies.

Staying in the dormitory of a local college close to the course, I settled into St. Andrews and became familiar with Tom's personality and game. When a caddie first works with a player, one of the first things he or she must do is learn the player's "yardages," just how far he or she hits each club under ideal circumstances. Crucial to properly "clubbing" a player, a caddie not familiar with his or her player's yardages would be quickly out of a job due to bad advice. For instance, clubbing Cory Pavin would be a totally different experience than clubbing Tiger Woods, who might hit 3-wood, wedge when Cory is hitting driver, 6-iron. Though a player will quickly let you know what his or her yardages are, a responsible caddie will always verify the figures on the practice tee.

Besides knowing Tom's yardages, I had to learn his strengths and weaknesses and with what clubs and shots he felt most confident. Virtually the first Tour player to regularly use a lob wedge, Tom had a keen short game and implicitly trusted his game inside of one hundred yards. Tom isn't the longest driver on Tour, but he makes up for it with accuracy and strategic positioning of the ball.

Working with Tom that week turned out to be easy and enlightening. He was a snap to club and had a keen, strategic golf mind that made my job simple, even in the challenging environs of St. Andrews, where the ever-present wind always dictates tactics. Tom fortunately had all of the necessary shots, including the ability to keep the ball low, work it into the wind, and bump-and-run it into wind-quickened greens. Though the players I had worked with up to that point had all been talented and capable, Tom was definitely of a different caliber. I felt as if I'd jumped out of a Ford and into a Ferrari. It was a feeling I could easily learn to like.

During this British Open, I learned a lot about what made Tom Kite a great competitor. Throughout his career, he's had the ability to truly take the game one shot at a time and to remain relatively calm and upbeat, understanding that lament over a bad shot is the best way to ruin the next. He's nearly always cool and methodical, with an almost professorial work ethic. Few players have ever worked harder on the game than Tom, who is often found practicing when others are long gone.

We played the Open well and had had a chance to win on Sunday. Unfortunately, Tom didn't make enough birdies down the stretch and wound up tied for second place, along with fellow Harvey Penick disciple Ben Crenshaw, as well as Simon Owen and Raymond Floyd. Back in 1978, tieing for second at the Open paid a whopping fourteen thousand dollars; my cut of that covered expenses, with a wee bit more to spare. What was more valuable to me, though, was that I had laid down the foundations of a good working relationship with one of golf's greatest players.

In 1980, while still officially caddying for Lon Hinkle, I was informed by him that he would be using his brother-in-law for that year's British Open. Disappointed at losing the opportunity to go overseas again, I checked around to see if any players were in need of a caddie. As luck would have it, Tom Kite would be, just as he'd been two years prior. Disco, his regular caddie, did not want to go to Scotland (as he hadn't in 1978), causing Tom to search for a temporary replacement caddie. As we'd already worked the British Open together, Tom had no doubts about my abilities, and agreed to hire me on for the week of Europe's biggest tournament, at that point only a month or so away.

Two weeks before the British Open, however, I heard that Tom was contemplating a permanent change in caddies, despite finishing third (with Disco on his bag) at the U.S. Open just two weeks earlier. This was a disappointing blow for me, for if Tom was to replace Disco, the new permanent caddie would surely want to go to Scotland for the British Open, removing Tom's need for me, a mere substitute. Tom said nothing to me about any changes, though, so I uneasily went ahead and booked passage to Scotland.

Upon arriving at the course, I spotted, of all people, Disco, who had decided to go overseas after all. Seeing him made my heart sink; I'd thought that Tom had changed his mind again, and that the talk of him changing caddies might have been simply to convince Disco to come over after all. My horror turned to relief when I discovered that Disco had inexplicably come over to caddie for another player, Andy Bean, and that Tom still needed me. Disco's move may have upset Tom, because on Friday of tournament week, he walked up to me and simply said: "Welcome to the team, Mike." I had his bag full time, and not just for the British. I'd gone from having a few dollars in my pocket and hitching across the country, to caddying for one of the best golfers in the world. Our relationship has lasted twenty years, and is still going strong.

The Tours

Anyone crazy enough to actually consider trying his or her hand at professional caddying should know that there are a number of options available besides the PGA Tour, improving the odds of actually finding a bag. The PGA Tour is definitely the "bigs," though, as far as I'm concerned, not only from a money standpoint but also in terms of status and talent as well. Let's face it; these guys are good, and they show it every week. Those of you who have only watched the likes of Kite, Woods, Els, or Duval on television are missing the up-close perspective that can only be appreciated in person, at a tournament. Standing behind Tom two hundred yards out from a well-protected green, it never ceases to amaze me how he can pull a 4-iron, visualize the shot, then execute it the way you or I would an eighty-yard wedge shot. The accuracy, power, and consistency of the Tour players is mind-boggling and can't be fully appreciated on television. They are truly the cream of the crop and to land a job caddying for one of them is a rare opportunity indeed.

The LPGA Tour is another venue that provides caddies with regular work. Filled with talented female golfers from all walks of life, the LPGA has enjoyed quite a surge in popularity

of late, with the appearances of stars such as Annika Sorenstam, Karrie Webb, and Se Ri Pak, to name a few. Some golfing
fans I have spoken with enjoy watching the women play as
much or more than the men, mainly because the women hit the
ball distances that are much closer to the game the average
golfer plays. I know that I am much more likely to hit driver,
three-wood, nine-iron on a long par-5, rather than the driver,
middle-iron most PGA Tour players now hit. That game is
unreal and unapproachable by most; the women's game is more
familiar and therefore often more enjoyable to watch.

Unfortunately, events on the LPGA Tour have substantially
smaller purses than those of the PGA Tour, reflecting the
greater overall popularity and profitability of the men's game.
Though not necessarily fair, it is the reality of the business.
Consequently, caddies on the LPGA Tour do not make as much
money as their PGA Tour counterparts. A good number of the
LPGA players fail to crack the one hundred thousand dollar
barrier in a year; as most caddies get only five to ten percent of
a player's take, you can see the financial difficulty it creates.
Someone making less than ten thousand dollars in a year can't
raise a family, or do much of anything. Because of this, players
on all Tours with small purses often resort to using relatives or
friends as caddies to offset costs and to insure that someone
reliable will be there each week.

The Senior Tour provides caddies with another venue for
plying their skills. Not to be outdone by the PGA Tour players,
the top Senior player of 1997 and 1998, Hale Irwin, earned
more money than the top PGA Tour players of both years, Tiger

Woods and David Duval. Make no mistake; purses on the Senior Tour are high, making caddying for a successful Senior a potentially lucrative position. The number of successful players are fewer, however; only the top thirty or so on the money list are assured of their cards the following year, as opposed to one hundred twenty-five or more on the PGA Tour.

Those caddies who do make it onto the bag of a Senior Tour player get a new lease on life, much like the "over-fifty" players who could no longer compete effectively on the PGA Tour. Both caddies and players can and do work well into their sixties and sometimes even longer. At sixty-nine, Arnold Palmer is still making birdies and hitting the ball a mile. Sixty-four-year-old Gary Player just recently won the Senior British Open. Caddies, due to a lifetime of aerobic activity, generally stay in good shape and can often outlast their players' careers. Ernest "Creamy" Caroline, Palmer's caddie during his heyday, worked for nearly fifty years and still caddied well into his seventies. Angelo Argea, Jack Nicklaus's caddie for many years, also worked well into his later years and finally retired from caddying to open up a yardage book business out of southern Florida. Jack actually has Angelo create yardage books for many of the courses he now builds. Herman Mitchell, Lee Trevino's longtime caddie, Lee Lynch (the caddie on Al Geiberger's bag when he shot his famous record fifty-nine), and Roy Stone (the Tour's only Native-American caddie) all worked into their seventies. The current use of carts on the Senior circuit also makes it easier for caddies and players to continue competing well into their later years. Thus, caddies ready and willing to work past the age of retirement are provided that opportunity on the Senior Tour. The catch, of course, is that most of the Senior players come from PGA Tour ranks and bring their caddies with them onto the Senior circuit, severely limiting the number of openings. Some seniors even use their grown children as caddies, further limiting the chances of finding a bag.

The Buy.com Tour (originally the Nike Tour) is another venue where caddies can practice their trade. Acting as a proving ground for potential PGA Tour players, the Buy.com Tour can and does serve the same purpose for up-and-coming caddies, often friends or relatives of the young players grinding it out each week. Caddies working the Buy.com Tour make even less money than do those on the LPGA Tour due to substantially lower purses as well as the less consistent play of many of the golfers, a good number of whom do not last very long. A caddie's life on the Buy.com Tour is very much like what it used to be for PGA Tour caddies years ago, in that much of the traveling is done by car rather than plane. Many Buy.com Tour caddies end up carpooling all over the country, staying at the cheapest motels, and eating more greasy fast food than they might care to, all a result of the paltry amounts of money available. But just as it is a good proving ground for players, the Buy.com Tour is a good primer for those willing to give caddying a go. Also, players who do well enough on the Buy.com Tour to win a PGA Tour card will very often bring their caddies along with them, making all those greasy meals and roach-trap motels well worth it.

Caddies not able to find work on any of the four Tours have the option of finding a lesser player on one of the regional mini-tours across the country, staging grounds for players with hopes of one day being on one of the more lucrative tours. Most of these caddies make very little and are usually friends or relatives helping the player out on a temporary basis. Again, it is a start, albeit not a very lucrative one.

The European and Asian Tours are two other venues that can provide a caddie with work. Often a player not able to make it onto the PGA Tour (and not able to raise a family on Buy.com Tour earnings) will play in Europe, Japan, or some other part of Asia, where purses are closer to PGA Tour standards. Brian Watts is a perfect example; runner-up to Mark O'Meara at the 1998 British Open, he has been a leading money winner in Japan for some time and is only just now making a go of it on the PGA Tour.

Usually, players native to these other areas of the world will rarely hire an American caddie due to language and cultural differences, which can make communication difficult or impossible. Likewise, an American or Canadian player going overseas will most likely bring with him or her a caddie who speaks the same language and shares the same cultural mores. Under these circumstances, caddies and players tend to socialize off the course much more than do their counterparts at home.

Paupers, Kings, Caddies

A caddie derives inexplicable pleasure from waking up each week in a different Motel 6 or Roadway Inn and in comparing a Denny's Grand Slam breakfast in Akron, Ohio, with one in Austin, Texas. All professional "bag toters" (as old Roy Stone liked to call his fellow caddies) love the lure of the road, camaraderie with good friends, and the sense of rootlessness that exists, at least in the beginning of a career, before marriage and children catch up.

He or she probably smokes, drinks too much coffee, enjoys a beer or two (or three) every now and then, and knows how to live on a shoestring for a very long time. Most caddies can shoot a fair game of golf, and all can walk just about anybody into the ground. Caddies are gentlemen and lady rogues, independent travelers who have found their way into a select, rarified crowd that almost (but not completely) accepts them as one of their own. They are like rock star roadies who help make the show possible, all the while standing backstage, on the fringes of fame. Glad to play a part, caddies are well aware of their own transience and of their shadowy separation from golf's elite kingdom.

How Players and Caddies Team Up

The next time you open up your local newspaper, count the number of "Tour Caddies Wanted" ads listed in the classified section. Odds are you might find one or two in a lifetime. In other words, the supply of caddies has always far outstripped the demand. And unless the Tours drastically increase the number of players in competition, chances are it won't change soon.

Among all the Tours in the world, there probably exists a need for less than a thousand caddies, total. That's it. For every position that opens, there are probably hundreds of men and women ready to step into the role on a moment's notice. So how on Earth can someone find a bag?

Most caddies fall into the job accidentally or start on a temporary basis as a favor to a golfing friend or relative who, just starting out in the game, can only initially afford to pay a caddie room and board. For every Tiger Woods, Phil Mickelson, or David Duval, there are dozens of players struggling to make a living and keep their Tour cards. Beginning players on the smaller tours especially cannot afford to keep an experienced caddie on the payroll and more often than not call on the volunteer services of a brother, friend or spouse. Many caddies and players end up finding each other in this manner, letting sheer need and austerity dictate the pairing.

Many partnerships begin in this way. A caddie without a bag one week will show up at a tournament anyway, in hopes of finding a player in need. Some players never use a regular caddie and simply pick up whoever is available at the time. Kirk Triplett and Mark Calcavecchia often do this; both men will either choose an available caddie or simply have their wives caddie for them. In any event, if a player likes a temporary caddie's style and personality, the relationship could become a permanent one.

Word of mouth can help a caddie find work, provided he or she has an established reputation among the players. For instance, Mike "Fluff" Cowan, Tiger Woods's former caddie, had previously been the longtime partner of Peter Jacobson, a great player in his own right. Ironically, it was Peter who had suggested to Tiger during the 1996 U.S. Amateur at Pumpkin Ridge that he temporarily team up with Fluff for his first few professional tournaments, as Peter would be sitting out an injury for a few weeks. After a few tournaments, Fluff realized that Tiger was something special, and so he made one of the hardest decisions of his life. He left his boss and friend of sixteen years to try his luck with the boy wonder.

Because caddie/player relationships often do not last, a high turnover rate exists, creating good opportunities for a skilled caddie who is in the right place at the right time. The ideal situation is to find a good, solid player who likes your personality and caddying style and then try to keep that relationship going by winning. In many respects, I suppose the success rate of caddie/player relationships on the PGA Tour most closely resembles that of a marriage in the United States, of which nearly fifty percent now end in divorce. The moral of the story—when you find a good partner, stand by him (or her)!

On the Road Again

For me, one of the perks of the business has always been the lure of the road. My travels with Tom and other players I've caddied for have taken me to nearly every state in the Union, to Europe, Asia, and everywhere in between. I have caddied on courses in Africa where odd lizards or other creatures routinely bask out on the sunny fairways and where, every now and then, you hear an animal who could certainly eat you for lunch, if it had a mind to. While in Korea with Tom, I had the opportunity to go to the Demilitarized Zone, just a mile or so away from over a million armed, stoic North Korean soldiers. It was the only time I can recall in which most of the men surrounding me carried submachine guns instead of titanium drivers.

I can't think of many jobs that would have given me the same chance to explore the world and its people so thoroughly, other than perhaps flight attendant, army officer, or soccer star. The thought of spending the last twenty-eight years wearing a suit and being cooped up in an office sends shivers up my spine; I never could have done the nine-to-five grind and feel blessed that I've never had to.

The road is an integral part of the caddie's makeup and is what attracts most people to the job in the first place. Most caddies revel in the freedom the job provides and would literally suffocate to death inside the confines of a shirt and tie. We are outside working, in transit or at home, just as the golfers we work for are. We don't have to worry about pleasing hundreds of other people, just our players and ourselves. Who wouldn't enjoy such independence?

All caddies, in addition to loving the adventure and unpredictability of the road, love golf completely and would be playing competitively if they could. A few are just plain good, including Fluff Cowan, who has won the yearly caddies' tournament a few times; Ed Fletcher, who caddies for Leonard Thompson on the Senior Tour; Alan Copeland (nicknamed

"Nutsy"), who works for Phil Blackmar; and Eric Schwartz, former caddie to Cory Pavin. Most of us, though, can't break eighty on a good day, so we settle for being on the other side of the bag, the only other way to be involved in the game at its highest competitive level.

Whether traveling by car or plane, many caddies like to hit the road together, out of a sense of camaraderie or *esprit de corps*. Few caddies will actually travel with their players, who often have their families with them and may be coming from a different region of the country. I also think that many caddies just feel a bit more comfortable in the company of other caddies, not only out of friendship but also as a break from a work-like environment. In other words, after spending six to eight hours a day on the course with your boss, you might not want to spend more time together traveling or socializing. The road provides both player and caddie with that needed break; like a marriage, the best teams need a breather from each other every now and then in order to work well.

I've had loads of fun on the road. I remember driving nonstop from Cincinnati to Napa Valley, California, in two days, with three other crazed caddies in a beat-up station wagon and only one cassette tape to play for the entire trip. By the end of the trip we knew every song on the Eagles' "Desperado" album by heart. Or, running full bore up Interstate 5 California with my caddie buddy Shayne Grier in a borrowed Lincoln Continental, nearly running out of gas on the back roads of Yosemite National Park in the snow. I remember traveling with a caddie named Bob Wells, who, because of a bad stuttering problem, used to sing all of his conversations to avoid the problem. When he sang, the stuttering went away completely. Of course, he had a god-awful voice.

Learning the Ropes

There is no "Caddie University" handing out diplomas to eager, young bag toters. You basically jump (or get thrown) into the pond and hope that common sense, basic golf know-how, and some decent interpersonal skills will keep you afloat long enough to learn the finer points. I was lucky enough to start early and establish a good feel for the job before caddying on the Tour. Some caddies really do learn by the seat of their pants, however, relying greatly on the mentoring of the player or other caddies until "autopilot" kicks in. Even if a friend or relative of the player, a caddie on the Tour had better quickly learn the ropes.

I think anyone wanting to be a caddie on any level first needs to be able to play golf. Not necessarily great golf, but well enough so that he or she can understand the effects of good course management on the game. My handicap has been hovering around a 15 for, well, forever, it seems. Back in my college days I could regularly shoot in the high 70s to the low 80s, with my best score ever being a 72 on a par-69 course. Though my game has benefited tremendously from caddying for Tom all these years, the actual lack of playing time has hurt it. I get to play lots of golf during the winter break, but once the season gets rolling, it's hard to find the time to tee it up. Nevertheless, I play well enough to understand the importance of strategy and mindset; anyone wishing to carry a bag professionally had better be able to do the same.

Learning to caddie on a professional level really can't be learned before the fact, but is instead the greatest example of "on the job training" that I can think of. One literally gets thrown into the fire. Those who know the game well and get along with the player tend to survive. A lot depends on how tolerant the player is and on how much that player controls the decision-making process. If the player requires his or her caddie to merely carry the clubs and play cheerleader, then the learning process is often a smooth process. But if the player requires the caddie to participate in shotmaking decisions, conflicts could arise, ending with a disgruntled player and an unemployed caddie. The biggest variable affecting the caddie's survival, then, is the player's attitude and expectations.

The most important advice I could give a green caddie is to never give advice unless asked. Don't ever play the player's game for him or her, but be ready to contribute if asked. Don't initiate, just respond. And, as the round progresses, put yourself in the player's shoes; pretend it is you hitting the shots and think about what you would do.

Players are funny and unpredictable. Some place no blame on the caddie, while others stand ready to crucify and lay blame anywhere else but on themselves. Many players want a cheerleader on the bag and expect a neverending stream of positive, complimentary comments from the caddie, in an effort to boost morale and create a positive mindset. Others require as little of that as possible and desire a "speak when spoken to" type of relationship on the course. I have worked for both types of players and prefer not having to be a "rah-rah" caddie. I am quiet by nature, so being a supportive chatterbox isn't easy for me. Besides, a player who requires constant praise and emotional support often turns out to be a streaky player whose game hinges on mood and emotion. The best players are able to enter into an emotionless state of mind, not letting anger (or joy) affect play. When Tom is playing well, he controls his emotions superbly. Jack Nicklaus has probably been the best at turning off all emotion and becoming a strategic golfing machine, requiring little emotional support from his caddie.

That said, a caddie has to become the type of bag handler that the player desires. You have to go with his or her desires and give what is needed. The longest player/caddie relationships always result when both individuals share the same basic personality traits; mixing a boisterous, opinionated caddie with a quiet, calculating player usually means disaster. Tom and I tend to be both quiet and introspective; I believe this to be the secret to the longevity of our relationship.

Going for a Walk

I've probably walked ten or fifteen thousand miles of fairways during my time as a caddie. Maybe more—I'm not quite sure. And for every one of those miles, I had a full-sized bag stuffed with forty-odd pounds of golfing equipment and clothing strapped to my back. All in all, an interesting way to stay healthy, I'd say. Walking all those miles for Tom and the others has kept me trim and aerobically fit, thanks not only to the miles but to the hills as well. When you factor in the wind, rain, cold, and heat, I'd say I've developed into quite the mountain goat.

Anyone thinking about becoming a caddie better have great powers of endurance before trying out. I can guarantee that grabbing a Tour bag and setting off on a four-day, 72-hole journey will take the uninitiated by storm, to say the least. Blisters, muscle cramps and pulls, backaches, heatstroke, and just plain exhaustion await the inexperienced. Many fill-in caddies have suffered these unfortunate consequences. Most of them just don't have the proper conditioning, which involves not only aerobic fitness but ample upper-body strength as well. Well-meaning friends or family members who volunteer to help out for a week almost always go home nursing a sore body and a slightly bruised pride.

Apart from the sheer challenge of walking all those miles, a caddie needs to deal with the elements on a daily basis. The weather is always very unpredictable. Often we compete in windy, cold weather, particularly during the early part of the season. Rain, of course, is an ever-present and particularly miserable threat. Tour rules require the players to compete during rain, unless the greens become unplayable or if lightning becomes a threat.

The caddie's job becomes much busier in the rain. The number-one responsibility is keeping the grips dry. Nothing else, not even the player, gets as much attention. When you see a caddie holding an umbrella over his or her player during the pre-shot routine, it's not out of a desire to please the player but rather to keep his or her hands, gloves, and grips as dry as possible. A player who cannot maintain a dry connection to the club risks a disastrous and embarrassing shot. More than once I have seen a soaking wet club slip from the hands of a humiliated pro and fly farther than the ball. So when Tom hands me a wet club, I dry it off with a towel, then quickly slip it back into the bag, which has a zippered waterproof cover. Tournament sponsors are usually good at providing us with as many towels as needed, which can often be in high demand during a heavy rain. The player normally removes his or her glove as well, hanging it from the spokes of the umbrella to keep it as dry as possible.

Most caddies don't look like bodybuilders, and believe me, we're not. Some of us have bellies, while others are as skinny as pencils. All of us are capable of walking forever, though. A few caddies work out with weights, while others jog quite a bit. I stay in shape by caddying and playing golf, period, like most other bag handlers. It's worked for over thirty years, and I'm not about to change now.

Fuel

Any caddie (or player for that matter) who doesn't eat and drink during a round is nuts, in my opinion. When you are out there for four or five hours, your body is going to burn lots of its reserve energy and use up much of its fluid reserves. Those caddies and players who take the camel route and don't eat at least a piece of fruit and drink a quart of water end up feeling it by the turn, believe me. When I caddie for Tom, I always eat a light breakfast, then take along a banana or an apple, as well as a water bottle for both of us. Hot, humid weather especially takes the stuffing right out of you, particularly on hilly courses. Temperatures in Florida, Texas, Arizona, or Nevada can climb as high as one hundred degrees; without enough water, a caddie or player could collapse from heat exhaustion. If there is one piece of advice I could give amateur golfers, it would be to eat a banana and drink at least a quart of water during a round.

Caddies on the pro Tour do not drink liquor during a round. If they did, they'd get fired pretty darned quick. Alcohol impairs your judgment, saps you of energy, and dehydrates you. Any amateur players out there who drink a few beers during a round could probably pick up three or four strokes just by leaving the brew behind and replacing it with water or fruit juice. The easiest way to lose a Nassau bet is to drink it up on the course.

Where Do All the Caddies Go?

There is no retirement home for aged caddies. Nor is there a pension plan or any kind of PGA Tour-supported caddie fund of any type. All of us are considered independent contractors and as such must plan for our own retirement. Many, of course, never really do, mostly a result of not making enough year to year to put a sizable amount away for investment. Many caddies just keep working until their bodies can't cut it anymore, then try to make it on social security. A caddie lucky enough to team up with a Nicklaus, Kite, Woods, Norman, or Couples will, of course, have made enough over the years to have hopefully put away a good chunk of change in an interest-bearing account. Though I am not going to buy a yacht anytime soon, I won't have to worry about living my Golden years in an efficiency apartment in the slums of Miami. Thanks, Tom. Caddies for players who don't rake in the cash have a harder time with retirement and often have to work far into old age at menial jobs in order to survive.

Caddies on the Tour lucky enough to have been with a successful player have the comfort of knowing that the Senior Tour, with its comfy golf carts, looms ahead of them. No longer required to walk twenty-five miles each week, caddies can work well into their seventies without a problem. Tour players almost always take their caddies with them to the Senior Tour, so the word "retirement" really doesn't mean a whole lot to one of these lucky loopers.

The Professional Tour Caddies Association (PTCA) is working on trying to get some sort of pension plan going for Tour caddies, so that those less fortunate might have something to fall back on other than that tiny social security check, which might cover rent and a meal, if you're lucky.

Some caddies just disappear. Used to a very independent lifestyle, lots of them never put down roots and might not have any family around to help out when old age sets in. I am lucky enough to have my great wife Rene, who will (I hope) take care of me when I can no longer chew my food or hit a 7-iron more than a hundred yards. Many caddies do not marry, though, and end up living a pretty austere life after leaving the game. Some players do help out, but the majority do not have any kind of retirement plan set up for their caddies, even for those they have been with for many years. To be fair, it is hard enough for most of the players to survive out there without having to worry about supporting their retiring caddies. The bottom line is that every caddie is a sole proprietor whose future depends on his or her business smarts. Some get lucky and find a Tom Kite, while others less fortunate hitch rides with a series of falling stars and end up with nothing but bittersweet memories.

PART TWO

The Caddie/Player Relationship

Marriage, PGA Style

It used to be that couples in the United States got married young, had a flock of kids, and stayed together forever, weathering just about any storm that came their way. Today a marriage has about as good a chance of succeeding as a first novel. Sign of the times, I suppose. People don't have the same expectations anymore, or else can't tolerate the slightest difference of opinion on anything. Sadly, more than half of the marriages end up in divorce court.

The success rate for caddie/player relationships on Tour mirrors that of marriages in this country and might even be a hair worse. Some do last (as evidenced by Tom and I), but many fizzle, fade, or self-destruct, mainly due to personality differences, inexperience, ineptitude, superstition, scapegoating, or sheer intolerance on the part of the player. Curiously, this unique sporting relationship more closely resembles sexist marriages from the fifties, with the husband (read "player") in charge and the wife (read "caddie") keeping house and managing the domestic essentials. The player calls the shots, makes the money, and defines the course of the relationship, with the caddie willingly (or unwillingly) acquiescing to the player's demands and desires. The caddie has few alternatives and has to surrender to the whimsy of the player, who, though often right, can also be very wrong at times. But just as the customer is always right, so is the player. Chauvinistic, perhaps, but true. A caddie must always bow to the player's desires, moods, and needs and must be ready to bear the brunt of the responsibility for a bad shot, even if the player was the sole cause of it. Bottom line: it ain't always a picnic out there.

Don't get me wrong—some caddie/player relationships have the perfect chemistry. Take, for example, Nick Price and Jeff "Squeaky" Medlen, may he rest in peace. I don't think a better pairing of personalities and talent ever existed on the golf course before. Nick and Squeaky were truly a perfect match; a super talent with uncanny technique, poise, and attitude and a wily, supportive, hardworking right-hand man with a great personality and an unparalleled drive to win. Squeaky always used to get to the course earlier than anyone to pace off yardages and familiarize himself with the hazards and the overall design of the course. Unlike other player/caddie relationships, Nick and Squeaky were close friends, often socializing with each other off the course. Squeaky had worked with Freddie Couples for a while, but he really found a home with Nick. Together, they dominated the Tour back in the mid-nineties, with Nick winning two majors and player of the year honors in 1994. I considered Squeaky a good friend and miss him much, as do all of us. I know that a day doesn't go by that Nick does not think of him fondly.

The Relationship

The success of the caddie/player relationship depends primarily on the caddie winning the confidence of his or her player and on having a personality as similar to the player's as possible. Any player I've ever carried for needed to know immediately that I had good decision-making abilities and the desire to go that extra yard in preparing for a tournament. Above all, I had to be there when needed, not only physically but emotionally as well. Competitive golfers are so, so good at what they do; often the difference between winning and missing a cut is more a question of attitude and self-confidence than of raw talent. Having an experienced, supportive caddie on your side can often mean the difference between first and tenth place, simply due to the intangible influences a savvy, tuned-in caddie can have. I think Tom summed it up well in the beginning of our relationship when he said, "Mike, I need a friend out there."

Some rookie players will need to depend quite a bit on a seasoned caddie's advice and experience—Tiger wasn't paired with Fluff for nothing. A wily old caddie (like me) can do wonders for a player right out of Q-school, particularly because of his or her ability to share course knowledge, the factor rookies most sorely lack. The first year on Tour can be confusing for many players, even the gifted ones; having a seasoned bag handler along can often mean the difference between winning or going home Friday night.

When a player is on, he or she could probably use a ten-year-old caddie and still win. It is when a player is grinding, though, that a good caddie shows his or her mettle. Under these circumstances, the caddie must remain on an even keel and, at the same time, find a way to lift the player out of his or her funk. You have to be positive but not emotional, and supportive without being patronizing. Above all, a good caddie can never mope, become negative, or *ever* criticize a player.

Some players are eminently fair and civil with their caddies, whereas others can be downright unfair, blaming their own failed shots on the caddie, even if he or she had no input at all. I believe psychologists call it "displacement behavior." It can become an almost masochistic experience for a caddie, particularly if the player has done poorly all season and is subconsciously hunting around for a defenseless scapegoat. As none of us want to be fired, most caddies will swallow large and bitter pills in an attempt to weather the player's storm. If it goes on too long, though, most of us will start looking for another ride. When a player gets into this kind of predatory, hostile mode, he or she will often fire the caddie anyway, thinking that any change will be for the better.

I have had better luck than that. With few exceptions, my players have been eminently fair with me. Sure, some have lost their cool, but most have never blamed me for their own shortcomings. Tom is very fair and honest; right at the beginning of our relationship, he told me up front that every now and then he might lose his cool and take a bad shot out on me, and that I shouldn't take it personally, that he was just venting. I appreciated him telling me that and can count on one hand the times he's unfairly laid the blame on me. Again, I've been lucky enough to have enjoyed the company of one of the most celebrated and respected gentlemen golf has ever known. In other words, I have had it pretty easy with Tom, a classy guy to say the least.

A good caddie can sense what a player needs or wants before asked. I know Tom's game so well that I can predict with ninety percent certainty what club he is going to need. Some inventive short game shots of his have over the years caught me off-guard, though. For instance, during the first round of the 1998 PGA Championship at Sahalee Country Club in Redmond, Washington, Tom hit his drive on the par-4 3rd hole into a mass of huge, tangled, pine needle-covered tree roots. His approach shot to the green was one that most amateurs would have been terrified of; the ball was sitting about 120 yards short of the green, on the left side of the fairway. Only a small goal-post clearing formed by two huge cedar trunks existed, with the green at least fifty feet below his feet. From there, I honestly didn't think I could have hit the green with a hunting rifle. Any high wedge shot from there would have caught the trees instantly, and a standard middle-iron shot would have flown the green. I wasn't about to hazard a guess at this one. Tom ended up choosing a 7-iron and picked the ball cleanly out of the poor lie with a steep three-quarter swing, punting it right through the cedar goal posts and landing it well short of the green, letting it scoot its way down. The ball rolled through the green into a back bunker, and Tom ended up with an excellent bogie after two-putting from eight feet.

My relationship with Tom has really helped improve my game. We actually get to play a few rounds together each year. He's a blast to play with and has helped me tremendously with my own course management skills as well as with my swing. Playing with him is like getting a boxing lesson from Muhammad Ali, minus the concussion and the poetry. In turn, as my own game improves, so does my ability to be an effective caddie.

Most players and their caddies try very hard to create a sedate "bubble" of calmness around them when competing in a tournament. To help accomplish that, I have to make Tom's day as automatic and carefree as possible. That means keeping all the equipment in perfect condition, making sure I am right where I'm needed, and, above all, doing my pre-tournament homework, knowing yardages, pin placements, and course design. Any doubt he has about distance to a pin or a hazard can erode confidence. My job is to eliminate as many confidence-sapping situations as possible so that he can be clear of mind. Without that, negative thoughts can and do seep in, inevitably causing a chain reaction of bad shots. Bad thoughts are like viruses to a Tour player; they multiply until the host is incapacitated. Only rest and elimination of the invading "contagion" can cure the problem. My job is largely preventative—as

Tom's caddie, I need to act as an "antibody," searching out and killing off any potentially game-killing negative thoughts or conditions before they get a chance to infect my host player and render him ineffective.

If Tom asks, I will watch his swing and give him feedback on areas with which he is most concerned. In addition, I keep Tom appraised of the time so that he doesn't have to feel that pressure. He lets me worry about getting us to the tee and just concentrates on entering into his "zone."

Business First

Every caddie must first establish some type of agreement with his or her player regarding salary, commission, and bonuses. Almost all of these agreements are verbal, not written; it is one of those curious golfing traditions that has endured over the decades and remains the norm for all but the slim minority. Traditionally, players have always wanted to reserve the option of letting a caddie go if he or she is not working out, and a written contract would restrict that ability and perhaps interfere with a player's concentration. In effect, a caddie can be fired on the spot. Dave Woosely, caddie to Chip Beck for nearly six years, got an unexpected phone call from his employer one day a few years ago, informing him of his immediate dismissal. No advance notice, no face-to-face explanation. Just a phone call. Since no written contract existed, there was nothing he could do.

Still, caddies have traditionally gone along with the absence of a written contract, as they generally want to be as unencumbered as possible. Having to stay with a player who continually misses cuts would spell disaster for most caddies, who would prefer to have the option of looking for a more profitable bag. Five or ten percent of nothing is, after all, nothing, which is rather hard to live on.

Most caddies generally receive a guaranteed weekly salary of about six hundred dollars throughout the season. Top players will pay a bit more than that, perhaps seven hundred to nine hundred dollars per week, with one or two paying as high as twelve hundred dollars. When a player takes a month off, though, his or her caddie gets nothing. From this salary, caddies normally must pay their own expenses, including hotel accommodations, food, and travel. Exceptions abound from relationship to relationship, however. For instance, some players will pay a caddie's airfare and hotel accommodations for tournaments in Europe, Asia, or some other far-off destination. Generally speaking, though, caddies pay their own way from their weekly salaries.

On top of the weekly salary, a caddie will receive a percent of the player's winnings, normally around five to seven percent depending on what place they finished. In addition, if the player actually wins a tournament, that amount often goes up to ten percent. This is where a caddie makes his or her living; the salary really only goes toward expenses. By doing the math, you can see the incentive every caddie has for helping his or her player to victory. A few caddies each year can actually make six figures, if they are lucky enough to be with one of the top five money winners for the season. In 1999, with purses going up by about forty percent, a number of caddies will be making some serious money.

Increasingly, due to the efforts of the Professional Tour Caddies Association, caddies have begun to land endorsement deals. If you look closely, you now can often see sponsor's logos on caddies' visors, hats, or shirts. If it works for the players, it can work for caddies, too, who appear on camera nearly as often. This additional income really helps make ends meet and can make a big difference at the end of the year.

Of course, most caddies do not get rich. They make a decent living in a profession without much job security and stay with it partly out of love for the game, and also because the thought of wearing a tie and sitting on their butts all day literally gives them the shakes.

Lessons Learned

During the U.S. Open at Oak Hill in 1989, Tom and I both learned a valuable golfing lesson. He'd been playing well all week and was as patient and focused as I'd ever seen him. In the last round, he had a three-shot lead after four holes, but at the fifth hole he blocked his tee shot right. We both watched in horror as the ball rolled right into a creek.

Tom stayed calm. We discussed our options and decided to play for bogey, not wanting to risk an Open championship on a heroic but costly recovery shot. Nevertheless, he ended up tripling the hole, something he might do once a year, if that. During the rest of the round, Tom didn't press or panic, but his swing just wasn't there anymore. The fickle gods of golf had just taken it away from him and denied him a major victory.

After the loss, Tom began to work on correcting the flaw in his swing, an annoying block that caused the ball to go right, without drawing at all. Famous for his work ethic, Tom worked on the problem, which was related to the release of the club head, religiously for the next few weeks and solved it. He went on to win the Nabisco Tournament later that season and ended up with the money title for 1989.

Afterward, we discussed the loss at the Open and agreed that it hadn't been mental or strategic errors but simply a flawed swing that had lost it for us. Being able to clearly identify what the problem was helped Tom keep the rest of his game intact. Many players are not able to focus on the essential problem and begin tinkering with other aspects of their games instead, often resulting in a meltdown of their entire game. By confidently identifying Tom's lack of proper release as the culprit, we were able to avoid disaster.

Caddies and players alike learn tremendous lessons from both their victories and defeats on Tour. For instance, the first few rounds that I caddied on Rocky Mountain area courses were truly educational, to say the least. At nearly one mile above sea level, the air is significantly thinner than normal, resulting in shots that routinely travel ten to fifteen percent farther than usual. A rookie player/caddie duo might not initially make the necessary adjustments for club selection, resulting in a series of embarrassing approach shots, many of which fly right into the crowds surrounding the greens. Believe me, this kind of experience teaches one to respect the laws of physics very, very quickly.

The same goes for playing golf on courses overseas. My first few experiences on European courses, for example, were highly educational. Here in the United States, Tour players and caddies have all become used to nearly perfect conditions. Fairways and greens are normally more lush and manicured far better than those in Europe, where players have to deal with brown, fast fairways, wind-hardened greens, and a host of other imperfections that stateside courses do not tolerate. Tom loves less than perfect conditions and always feels more confident when the wind is howling. He knows that his experience playing on windy Texas courses has given him the upper hand on other players; we always feel a surge of confidence when the wind is blowing and value the years of experience that helped us cultivate that feeling.

The lesson most amateur golfers can derive from this is to try to vary the conditions you play in as much as possible, instead of playing on the same home course every time. Doing so will improve your "golfing computer" and make future rounds on unknown courses much easier.

Over the years, Tom and I have played all of the world's famous courses dozens of times. I know these courses' unique idiosyncrasies, from Augusta's lightning-fast undulating greens to Pebble Beach's sobering wind and water grinches. Knowing the subtle slopes of fairway landing areas or the locations of troublesome trees, ridges, and swales makes my job (and Tom's) much easier. Rookie players and caddies have to learn and remember all these hundreds of tidbits of information as quickly as possible if they are to survive and win on Tour. If the player or caddie has experience, the odds of success are higher than if both are green, wide-eyed newcomers. If both caddie and player are veterans, the odds of victory go way up.

Moving On: The End of a Caddie/ Player Relationship

Golfers are in the business of winning and making as much money as possible each year. If they do not stay in the top one hundred twenty-five on the money list each year, they are off the Tour, period. Athletes in all other sports have multi-million dollar deals with the franchises they play for, and as long as the contract is in effect, they are guaranteed a salary and a place on the team, regardless of how they perform. Pro golfers do not get guarantees; they are independent contractors who must produce every single week. Miss the cut and you don't get paid. Because of this, they have to constantly evaluate every factor of their games, from equipment selection, swing flaws, and physical conditioning to tournament scheduling or even time spent practicing.

One factor that can be easily and quickly changed by a

player is his or her choice of caddie. If a player's game suddenly "goes south," for instance, he or she, in a desperate search for a solution, might decide to change caddies in an attempt to inject some new input into the equation. Cory Pavin, for example, whose game has suffered tremendously over the past few years, just recently fired his longtime caddie Eric Schwartz in an attempt to turn things around. It is not that he necessarily thought that Eric was the cause of the slump, but rather that his choice of caddie is one of the sole factors he had complete control over. So, due in part to superstition or frustration, some caddies get the heave-ho in favor of new blood.

Other caddies get axed because of ineptitude, plain and simple. Tour players expect a high level of talent and responsibility from their caddies. Any looper who consistently shows up late or unprepared, or gives bad input, is asking for a pink slip. Acting disrespectfully or giving incorrect yardages will nearly always result in dismissal (even if the caddie is married to the player).

Sometimes age or health reasons end a caddie's career. If a caddie is no longer able to keep up, the player really has no other option but to let him or her go. Injuries can unfairly cause a change of caddie; a broken leg or serious surgical procedure, for example, can lay a caddie up for an entire season. The player has no option but to replace the person, unintentionally causing a new relationship to blossom. The original caddie eventually heals, only to find the position filled. Fair, no. Reality, yes.

Sometimes a caddie/player relationship ends by the choice

of the caddie. Fluff Cowan, for example, switched from Peter Jacobson to Tiger Woods, for obvious reasons. Other caddies simply decide to take a job in a less unpredictable, more secure field. Who can blame them? Still others decide to retire and bask in the Florida sun for the rest of their lives. If they can afford that option, then by all means, congratulations to them!

PART THREE

Playing the Game

Caddie Sense's main purpose is to act as your own private Tour caddie. This section will do just that; all you need do is sit back and allow me to share with you the skills and experience I have acquired during my many years on Tour with Tom Kite and others. I will cover everything from equipment and set-up positions to course strategy, common amateur mistakes, how the pros practice and prepare, and much, much more. Sit back, relax, and let me carry your bag for a while.

Equipment Basics

All golfers, amateurs and professionals alike, must use the proper equipment if they are to succeed on the course. Using the wrong club or ball, wearing improper clothing, or improperly maintaining the right equipment can all lead to failure on the course. Tour players, who often win or lose major tournaments by one shot, strive to fine-tune their golfing tools to a much higher degree than do most amateurs in an attempt to utilize every possible advantage. To that end, they spend a good amount of time and effort choosing the proper equipment and having that equipment adjusted to meet their individual needs.

Let's use Tom Kite as an example. Always very precise and particular about his equipment, Tom had until just recently used Hogan clubs but has now decided to switch over to Titleist products. He has always preferred forged blades to perimeter-weighted, investment-cast irons, due to the greater feedback and "workability" factors. Most pros use blades for these same reasons; as they are less forgiving on off-center hits, the player knows when he or she has missed the "sweet spot," even by a half-inch. Perimeter-weighted, investment-cast irons, designed to be more forgiving on off-center hits, do not give the pro player the same vibrational warnings. If you or I hit an off-center shot with our perimeter-weighted Callaways or Taylormades, the ball still goes relatively straight, with only a few percent reduction in distance. A reduction of only a few yards for the pro player, though, can mean disaster; consequently, they want to know immediately when they have missed that sweet spot. When you mis-hit a blade, the resulting vibrations sent up the shaft and into your hands really let you know that you missed it.

In addition, a forged blade in the right hands can work wonders on ball flight. If Tom needs to hit a high draw or a low fade, he knows he can do it reliably with a blade. Cast irons are not quite as effective at this—remember, they are designed for the typical amateur, who is forever trying to *rid* his or her game of hooks or slices. Perimeter-weighted clubs are designed to hit the ball straighter, something a pro rarely does or ever wants to do.

Lastly, pros prefer forged blades because they prefer the softer steel and because the club head lie or loft angles can be more easily adjusted if necessary. Investment-cast, perimeter-weighted irons cannot be adjusted nearly as much, as the metal is much harder and brittle. Pros like to tinker with these things and can do so more easily with blades.

Tom was one of the last Tour players to switch over to a metal-headed driver. He loved the feel of the older clubs and felt he was able to control his tee shots better with wood, due in part to the older clubs generating more "gear effect," a phenomenon that allows a toe-hit or heel-hit tee shot to fly straighter. The more rounded face of a quality persimmon driver head tends to cancel out slice or hook spin. Tom had a hard time finding a metal wood that could produce any gear effect at all. Due to their relatively flat faces, these new clubs caused a toe-hit shot to go right and a heel-hit shot to go left. Eventually, though, Tom could not ignore the significant advantage in distance that these new metal-headed drivers could produce. He finally found a Big Bertha that not only added nearly twenty yards to his drives but also provided him with some of the gear-effect phenomenon he had enjoyed with persimmon. Just recently, Tom switched to a Titleist 975 driver with 7.5 degrees of loft and a 46-inch stiff shaft, a club he feels has just as much feel as any old persimmon, with much more distance. He hits his drives farther now than he did fifteen years ago.

In addition to the Titleist driver and irons, Tom uses a Titleist metal 3-wood and has just recently replaced his persimmon 4-wood with a 17-degree Titleist metal wood. He feels that this club approximates the soft feel he had with his persimmon 4-wood. With his driver and 3-wood, Tom wants the ball to come off the face as hot as possible, for maximum distance. But with the 4-wood, control, not distance, is Tom's priority. He tried a number of metal 4-woods before finally putting the Titleist into his bag.

Tom's irons differ from other players in an interesting way. He carries 3-iron through a 52-degree pitching wedge, a 56-degree sand wedge, and a 60-degree lob wedge. Back in 1980, Tom began to chart his wedge shots, trying to determine if there was any way to improve his accuracy. With the help of his wife Christy, he painstakingly recorded all of his wedge shots over several months and discovered that distance control, not accuracy, was the major issue. Finding that he was very often left with "in-between" wedge shots, Tom decided that a third wedge was needed and was the first Tour player to begin using one. Eventually deciding on a 33.25-inch, 60-degree wedge, Tom could hit it exactly 75 yards with a full swing, just the distance he was looking for. Most players, including Tom, feel that sticking to a full swing is more precise than throttling back to a three-quarter or half swing, which often produces shots of varying distance. By now being able to use the exact same swing with every club, Tom solved his distance problems. To reinforce his decision, we found that after one year of using the 60-degree wedge (or "finesse" wedge, as he calls it), Tom's stroke average went down by a *full stroke*, a rare and valuable occurrence on Tour. Try adding that third wedge; it just may lower your scores too.

To make room for the extra wedge, Tom had to lose a club. Thinking that he made fewer birdies with his 2-iron than his wedges, he decided to drop it from his bag. To compensate for the loss, Tom had the lofts on his 3- and 4-irons made a bit stronger. That move, combined with the 4-wood, fills all of his gaps. The new set-up has allowed Tom to make many birdies on par-5 holes and short par-4s. And on Tour, birdie is the word.

The lesson that the average player can learn from this is not to be afraid to experiment with the clubs in your bag. Most amateurs only experiment with drivers, fairway woods, and putters and spend far less time perfecting their wedge games. Remember that wedges are your scoring clubs; trying to properly fill your yardage gaps from 125 yards and in will definitely improve your scores. If you can confidently step up to your ball and hit a full shot from 75, 100 or 125 yards instead of having to throttle back on a pitching wedge (or clobbering a sand wedge), you will have a much better chance of nailing the green and making par.

Tom normally uses his Bullseye putter but occasionally changes over to a Ping or some other similar design when having putting troubles. Tour players often find that a simple change in putter can, for some mysterious reason, improve performance on the greens.

Back in the 1980s, Tom used a Wilson-designed golf ball, but then he changed over to a Titleist Tour Balata for the added feel and workability. Just recently, however, he has gone to a new ball, the Titleist Prestige, which is somewhere in between the Professional and the Tour Balata in performance and feel. He gets more distance without sacrificing much feel with this ball. Tour players generally prefer a high-spin, soft-cover ball to induce effective draws or fades, stop a ball on the green, and for the overall "feel" factor. The difference in feel between a Balata ball and a cheaper rock-hard distance ball is truly amazing and can be a real factor in scoring on the green. Tour players who spin the ball too much, however, often go to a ball with somewhat less spin to prevent the ball from backing up right past the pin and into trouble.

For the amateur player, using a high-spin, soft-cover ball might not be the best idea. Most average golfers constantly struggle with stubborn hooks or slices; using a soft, high-spin ball will grossly exaggerate these problems, often leaving you in the woods, water, or out-of-bounds off the tee. Also, shorter hitters will find that they lose as much as ten yards or more off the tee with a softer high-spin ball, as opposed to a two-piece distance ball. In addition, Balata-type balls cut easier and are more expensive; a high handicapper might end up losing twenty dollars' worth of balls in one round.

For this reason, I recommend that you experiment with some of the new two-piece, perimeter-weighted distance balls that have a soft yet durable surlyn cover, allowing you adequate distance, fairly low spin, and good feel on the putting green. When your game improves to the point where you are consistently hitting more than half of your fairways and greens, it might then be time to go to a higher spin ball. But until then, strive for control, a little extra distance, and durability.

Most pros on Tour ask their caddies for a new ball every three holes or so to entirely eliminate any chance of ball scuffs or cuts affecting shot outcomes. As the average player does not receive boxes of free balls every week, it would not be practical to expect you to change balls so often. Changing balls at the turn, however, might help marginally, if only to let you see a bright, shiny, flawless ball on the tee instead of a scuffed, bruised, dirty little orb. Golf is more psychological than any other sport, and you need to do anything necessary to create a positive mindset.

Before a typical round, while Tom is loosening up, I busy myself with the duties that every caddie must perform. I clean each grip and club head, get out a fresh glove for Tom, mark all of his balls with his distinctive mark (a red line beneath the Titleist logo), and check ball numbers with the other caddies in our group to insure that we aren't playing the same ones. You should always use a unique identifying mark on your ball to prevent some other player from accidentally (or purposely) hitting your ball, leaving you to look in vain for a ball that is no longer there. Don't just use a dot; put your initials on it, or a smiley face, or even a small design, such as a triangle or asterisk. This will prevent any possible confusion out there.

Once on the tee, I count Tom's clubs to insure we have fourteen, and I make one last check to see if we have everything, including a pin sheet, copy of the local rules, snacks, and equipment. Then we go off to battle.

Grip maintenance is one area in which a great disparity exists between pros and amateurs. Most average players rarely clean their grips off and almost never change them. In contrast, I clean off Tom's grips thoroughly before each round and regularly wipe them off during the round, particularly when wet or sloppy conditions exist. In addition, Tom replaces his grips *every three months*. Know any amateurs who do that? Probably not. You, of course, will not play as many rounds per year as Tom Kite. However, it is a good idea to change your grips at least once each season to maintain good control and a slight edge over your opponents. If you cannot do it yourself, your local pro shop or discount golf store can probably do it for you at a price of three to four dollars per club, an investment of less than fifty dollars (about the price of eighteen good balls). In the meantime, always wipe down each grip with a damp towel before each round, just as I do for Tom. In addition to cleaning them off, this practice will leave the grips feeling nice and tacky, allowing you good control over your swing.

Tom uses a quality Foot Joy or Titleist golf glove. During a competitive round, he always uses a new glove, but he also carries with him a few used gloves for practice. The fit and feel of your glove is a crucial factor in maintaining good contact with your club; take the time to properly fit yourself. The glove should fit snugly, with no bunching or folding of material. Also, avoid cheaper gloves made of thicker leather, as they will decrease feel. Let your glove dry off naturally; never use heat, as this will destroy the glove's feel and shrink it as well. When your glove gets to the point where it has the beginnings of a hole (usually on the pads of your hand) or has stretched out enough to cause folds in the palm or fingers, replace it. Try keeping a few old gloves around for practice sessions, saving your best glove for rounds that count.

The choice of shoes on Tour is no minor matter. The overwhelming concern for a pro player is maintaining a solid base during the swing. In order to do this, the spikes used must remain firmly planted. No slippage can be tolerated at all, for safety's sake, as well as for power and control. Many players have switched to soft spikes over the last few years, which seem to be marginally kinder to greens and give adequate traction under most conditions. Quite a few Tour players have decided to stay with traditional spikes, however; Tom feels that he gets better traction with them and doesn't see any reason to switch. Your overriding concern should be comfort and stability; don't skimp on a golf shoe, unless you don't mind blisters by the sixth hole. Check if your home course has recently disallowed metal spikes before buying them; recently, more and more courses are outlawing their use in an attempt to preserve the integrity of their greens.

Part of the uniqueness of golf is that any average player can buy and use the same equipment used by the pros. However, the clubs that Taylor-made, Callaway, or Top-Flite provides to their players have generally gone through a much higher level of quality control than identical clubs sold in retail stores. Loft and lie angles, shaft flex and length, and all other specifications are exact and adjusted to the player's desires. Tom will actually go to the factory and have his clubs ground to his unique specifications, and he has actually had over the years some input into the actual design of a set. In addition to being important advertising tools for the club manufacturers, input from pro golfers helps the companies decide which designs are working and which are not before the clubs ever hit the market. Most manufacturers have club representatives at each tournament and regularly offer players newly designed clubs to try out, free of charge, in an attempt to win them over and find out if the product performs well.

Tom doesn't change equipment unless absolutely necessary. "If it ain't broke, don't fix it" is a good rule for the average player as well; if you are playing well, stay with your clubs. Even if you have a problem with your game, avoid changing equipment right away, as you might make the problem even worse. Instead, go out and take a few lessons from a pro to get an impartial opinion of your game. If you have the wrong equipment, he or she will let you know.

No pro player uses clubs right off the rack, and you shouldn't either. The best thing you could do for your game is to have your clubs custom-fitted to your body and swing geometry. Club head lie and loft angles, shaft flex and length, and overall design can effect your ball flight tremendously and need to be taken into consideration right from the start. For instance, if the lie angle on your irons (the degree measurement made between the shaft and club head) is too upright for your stature, the toe of the club will stick up, causing lots of shots to fly left of the target. Also, if the flex of your shafts is too stiff, you will not get adequate distance and will find shots often blocked to the right, or else sliced.

Before buying a set of irons, find out if the retail store you frequent has custom-fitting available. If not, find a store that does. For only slightly more money, you will get a set of clubs that will allow you to hit the ball straighter and truer. The pros do it—why shouldn't you?

In addition, always try out clubs before buying them. Most stores will allow you to do this, either into a net or at a nearby range. As indoor nets really don't allow you to observe ball flight, I recommend you hit the club or clubs in question at a range before ever putting down a cent. Different clubs have differing ball flights; you need to choose one you are happy with.

Most pros constantly tinker with their equipment, and Tom is no exception. He loves to play around with clubs at home, changing grips, grinding club heads, or changing shafts. Arnold Palmer is another player who always loved to tinker, and has a complete workshop in his home for this very purpose. Club manufacturers provide repair trailers at every tournament, up to and including the Wednesday pro-am. Players needing repairs or adjustment can get them free at these trailers.

You can easily learn to do minor repairs and maintenance on your own clubs. Changing grips is one of the simpler things you can do, and it will save you money and give you a sense of accomplishment. Any book on club maintenance will be able to teach you how to replace your grips or even your club heads and shafts, if necessary.

Most players sign lucrative endorsement deals with several companies, who each pay the players to display company logos and also use their equipment (given to the players free of charge). Players today display almost as many company logos on their person and bag as a NASCAR entry. Next time you are watching Tiger, count how many swooshes he has on.

On Tour, players normally use a cavernous, full-sized Tour Bag, which serves not only as a container for forty or more pounds of equipment but also as another billboard for one of the pro's major sponsors. I, of course, put that bag into motion and take care of its organization during the week of a tournament. Unlike amateur players, the pros need to carry somewhat more equipment due in part to their need to deal appropriately with changes in weather. Let me first go through what equipment Tom always has on hand in his bag:

- Clubs, including driver, 3-wood, 4-wood, 3-PW, SW, LW, and putter
- Two or three sleeves of new balls
- Several new gloves, plus a few used ones
- Tees, extra spikes, and a spike wrench
- One large umbrella
- Rain gear
- At least one sweater during cold weather
- An extra hat, either cap-style or wide-brimmed

- Several towels
- A small first-aid kit, including Band-Aids and Advil
- Sunscreen
- Bag cover
- Rule book
- Fruits or snacks

In addition to these items, Tom might also carry mittens (for that occasional chilly round), an extra sweater or jacket, or even an extra pair of socks. On his person he carries a divot fixer, coins to mark his ball, a few tees, and whatever personal items he wants on him. Most players put wallets, watches, and jewelry into a small bag and keep it in one of the Tour bag's pockets to prevent any swing interference.

Infrequently, players will use a lighter summer bag during times of hot weather or when a spouse or relative is caddying. That doesn't happen often enough for me, though; I am usually stuck carrying that big old whale around some of the world's finest scenery.

Normally, a bag weighs less than forty pounds. That wasn't the case, though, during the U.S. Open back in 1992. The practice round had started out cool and foggy, causing players to don sweaters and rain gear. As the day wore on, however, it warmed up and dried out, causing most players to shed their protective gear. Unbeknownst to me, several of them were sneaking their sweaters and jackets into Tom's bag when I wasn't looking; by the end of the round, the bag probably weighed sixty pounds or more. Of course, I'd been so intent on checking yardages and other duties that I hardly noticed the extra burden until, one after another, the players began coming up to me and asking for their gear. Sweater after sweater and jacket after jacket was pulled from our bag's large compartment like so many Kleenex from a dispenser. Even my own player got a good laugh out of it and continues to do so to this day.

Know Thy Course

Tom and I have played many, many championship courses, over and over again. We probably know Augusta, Baltrusol, Congressional, St. Andrews, Pinehurst, and Pebble as well as you know your own home course. Most of the courses we play on don't change all that much over the years, allowing Tom and I to simply walk onto a course and know it like an old friend. For instance, at the 1999 Bob Hope Chrysler Classic, one of the courses used in the rotation was Indian Wells; I used an old, dog-eared 1986 yardage book for the course that day and found it to be completely accurate!

I have paced off distances to hazards, wandered in woods and rough, memorized hole designs, and played amateur meteorologist all over the world. I've studied grass, grain, sand, and slope, because doing so improved our chances of victory. Can you say that you have done the same on your home course?

How well do you know the courses that you regularly play on? For instance, if I asked you what type of grass is used on the fairways and greens, would you know? Would you know why having the answer to that question is important? What about prevailing winds, or drainage, or altitude? Many course factors combine to create a unique environment, one that exists only at that particular course. Luckily, you do not have to know dozens of courses, but only a few, or perhaps even just one.

Let's start with the basic design of the course. Is it a traditional parkland type, with lots of trees, continuous fairways, three- or four-inch rough, water, and out-of-bounds on many holes? Or is it a links-style course, with no trees, lots of wind, and high, wild grass or seaside gorse plants for rough? It could also be a desert course that encourages a target style of play, or a course with unusual conditions, such as in Hawaii (with its wind and extreme elevation changes) or in Colorado (with its altitude). Whatever the unique characteristics of your favorite course or courses are, you need to know how to deal with them in order to score well. Play a windy course as if it were a calm, protected one, and your scores will balloon like a sand wedge into a 30-mph wind. Ignore the effects of high altitude on distance, and you will find your ball flying greens like a poorly aimed mortar shell.

Even before you begin to study the basic layout of your course, become aware of several key fundamental factors:

- From which direction do the prevailing winds blow? Is this a constant, or do the winds often shift direction? Knowing this will help you immensely with club selection.
- What is the overriding weather pattern? Does the

area receive lots of rain each season, or is it relatively dry? Knowing this will help decide club selection and what type of shot to play.

- Does the course drain well or not? Knowing this will help you predict how much roll you will get on the fairways and how fast putts will roll on the greens.
- What level of maintenance can you expect at your course? How short do the groundskeepers cut the fairways and greens, and how often do they water? Knowing these facts will help you predict roll, speed, and lie.
- What is the elevation of your course? Knowing this will help you predict how far a shot will travel.
- At what level of difficulty is your course rated? Knowing this will put your performance into the proper perspective.

Knowing these fundamental factors will help you tremendously in understanding how your ball is behaving on the course and which strategies will work best for you.

You need to become intimately familiar with your home course. When the European players beat our American team (coached by Tom Kite) at the 1997 Ryder Cup matches at Valderrama, most analysts agreed that the Europeans' familiarity with the course was the deciding factor. You can hold the same advantage over those you play with, even if they play the same course just as often, by knowing how conditions and design affect the game.

Before you ever play a round, get hold of a yardage book or a scorecard that shows the basic layout of each hole. Then simply take it hole by hole. For example, looking at the first hole, you see that it is a 365-yard, dogleg-left par-4, with trees left and right and a small egg-shaped green protected in the front by two high-lipped bunkers and light rough in back. The pin is located right in the middle of the relatively flat green. The dogleg turn begins at about 185 yards out, with the narrow fairway canted to the left right at the elbow. The ideal shot calls for a nice draw right around that turn, leaving perhaps a middle or short iron to the green. A basic lesson here is to know that a draw is an almost mandatary strategy here if you are hitting driver or even 3-wood, unless you are a shorter hitter and do not hit your tee shots beyond 185 yards. If you hit your tee shots much farther than this (as many of you do), booming out a fade or even a straight shot will put you into the trees right, resulting in bogey or worse. That's not smart golf. If I were your caddie, I would advise you to set up on the left side of the tee box and hit a nice, soft draw, right around that corner. Or, if you didn't have that shot in your arsenal, I would simply advise that you lay up with a 3- or 4-iron, attempting to land the ball as close to the turn as possible without letting the roll run off the fairway. Simple, but those are two effective strategies for playing the hole.

You have succeeded in turning the corner and leaving yourself with a 135-yard approach shot. Now what? Look to your course knowledge again. What do you know about the green? Clearly, with bunkers guarding the entire front, you must not under-club or attempt a bump-and-run. With light rough behind the green, hitting it over slightly won't be nearly as punitive. Clearly, you need to fly your shot past the sand to the middle of the green. Normally a full 9-iron for you, you know that any error you make will land the ball into one of the bunkers. The smart thing to do would be to take a full swing with a gripped-down 8-iron instead. If you hit the ball too far, you will still be able to get it up and down from the light rough.

Though a fairly easy strategic challenge, this first-hole example shows how effective planning and course knowledge can help lower your score significantly. A player who just gets up to the tee and flails away with no course knowledge or game plan is certainly not going to be on the birdie train anytime soon.

Learn where all the hazards on your course are located. Bunkers, rough, water, high grass, trees, or other avoidable areas of a hole should all be programmed into your head before you even tee off. Know also the distances to all of these hazards from the tee and preferably from choice approach spots on the fairway. For instance, if you know that a fairway bunker is out at the 220-yard mark and you carry your driver about 225 yards, it's probably a good idea to throttle back to a 5-wood or 2-iron and lay up in front of the hazard. If, however, you routinely carry your driver 240 yards or more, it's probably safe to fly your ball right over the trap. Knowing precisely how far out a hazard is will make club and shot selection much easier and reduce the frustration factor greatly. Learning to play intelligently and conservatively will pay off for you in the end.

In addition to knowing where the hazards are, you need to take into consideration whether the hole in question has out-of-bounds bordering the fairway. Knowing this will allow you to avoid hitting your ball to that side. For instance, if the preferred landing area has rough left and out-of-bounds right, a slight draw would be a higher percentage shot than a fade to the right side of the fairway. If your basic shot is a fade, knowing about out-of-bounds right will cause you to aim well left; if the ball doesn't cut, it will still be in-bounds in the rough and not out-of-bounds right, causing you to suffer a stroke and distance penalty.

Become familiar with your course's topography. If, for instance, you step up to the 5th tee box and swipe a nice 3-wood out there about 235 yards, then find that the ball is sitting on a severe down-slope with a 145-yard shot left to the green, you have failed to plan efficiently. A downhill lie can be very tricky, as it usually creates a low, hot shot that is difficult to keep on the green. If you had taken note of the severe drop-off point beforehand, you would have taken driver and carried the ball past that down-slope onto a flatter area twenty yards beyond, or else throttled back to a 5-wood or 2-iron, landing the ball short of the drop-off, again on flat fairway. A 170-yard 4-iron off of a flat lie is almost always preferable to a 150-yard 6-iron off of a twenty-degree down-slope. The same advice would apply to severe up-slopes as well, though sometimes the additional loft put on a shot by this condition can actually help land a ball more softly. Avoiding side-hill lies is also important but is not always as easy to do, as it involves lateral direction control rather than just distance. You can control the distance of a shot far more consistently than you can its lateral direction, particularly when only ten or fifteen yards left or right are in question.

Knowing where each hazard or undesirable landing area is on your course allows you to "play the percentages," deciding which shot will have the highest probability of success. If a stand of tall cedars juts out into the left side of the fairway at around 260 yards, for example, you should know to avoid the left side of the fairway like the plague. Allowing your ball to land just short of the trees on the left side would prevent any reasonable approach shot to the green, as would putting your ball into the same trees. The higher percentage shot would be to fade a ball to the right side of the fairway, preferably just short of the offending grove, just in case the ball does not fade enough. The same principle applies to any hazard that lurks out there; taking the right club for proper distance control and hitting to the desirable side of the fairway effectively removes the threat. So instead of blindly walking up to the tee and swiping away, think about the design of the hole and decide on a target that avoids trouble.

Know the Greens

Just as you should learn all you can about fairway design and the hazards present there, so should you study the design of the greens on your course. Most greens that amateurs play on do not have the same difficult conditions present on the Tour, which has greens that tend to be much faster and more undulating. Many can still be quite challenging, however, and require just as much strategic thought as fairway play.

Knowing the topography of the greens will help you decide on what type of approach shot to hit. When Tom mulls over a 135-yard approach shot to a green, for instance, he considers many factors. First, the layout of the green itself is important. Does it slope from back to front, right to left, left to right, or front to back? If, for instance, the pin is set in fifteen feet off the front-middle portion of the green and the green slopes sharply back to front, Tom knows that the uphill path the ball will take after hitting the green will slow it down enough to prevent the ball from running too far past the hole. This allows him to target the hole fairly aggressively. The upward slope acts as a backstop. If the green slopes from front to back, however, it makes the shot much more challenging; even if Tom lands the ball well short of the pin, the ball will have a tendency to scoot well past the hole and perhaps into a back bunker. A green with a side-to-side slope will direct your approach shot left or right upon landing; knowing which way the slope goes in relation to your approach line will aid you in predicting where the ball will end up.

Study your greens carefully. Learn the slopes, the swales, and the shapes. Say, for example, you are eighty-five yards out from a flat, egg-shaped green, with the pin located in the narrow front section, which is bracketed by bunkers. This "sucker pin" location would be the target only if a championship was on the line or if the golfer shooting for it was a darned fool. The much better strategy would be to land the ball onto the wider back section of the green, then two-putt from there for par. Knowing that the green has this wider, safer area behind the pin would allow you to avoid an embarrassing bogey or worse. Never get suckered into shooting for a pin tucked in behind a bunker or a pond, for instance. Shoot for the open side and use a club that you can hit far enough to hit past the hazard, even if it means your ball ends up in light rough behind the green. You can still get up and down from there, but you won't from the pond and maybe not from the bunker. Remember, play for position and not the improbably heroic. Doing so has allowed cerebral, strategic, "percentage" golfers like Tom Kite and Jack Nicklaus to win many times on Tour.

In addition to shape and changes in green elevation, find out what direction the grain runs on your home course greens. Grain can affect the speed and the direction of your putt, and knowing which way it runs will help you decide on the proper line and speed. The grain on Bermuda greens affects putts more than grain on bent grass, but both need to be considered. Normally, Bermuda greens grow toward the setting sun or toward the nearest body of water; if you find yourself putting opposite the grain, you will lose at least five to ten percent of the speed you would have under normal, flat conditions. Conversely, putting with the grain will add speed, so adjust accordingly. Bent grass usually grows toward the drainage path, so allow for that when on this type of green. Generally, Bermuda grass is harder to play on than bent, both on and off the greens. Bermuda rough, for instance, is very wiry; balls landing in it tend to sink right down to the bottom and are very hard to get out.

Make sure that you always put in some time on the practice putting green before a round to get a feel for what speed the greens are running that day. Most courses maintain their practice greens with the same level of care and attention as with the greens on the course, and putting some practice balls will help you dial in the proper feel. Not doing so could result in some embarrassing three-putts on the first few holes.

Knowing how far the pin is to the front, back, and sides of each green will help you dial your approach shots in more precisely. When I calculate yardage for an approach shot, I pace off the distance from the sprinkler head to the ball. This distance is always to the front of the green. After getting our yardage to the front, I then refer to my trusty daily pin sheet (provided by Tour officials beforehand), which tells me precisely how far a pin is from the front, back, left, and right portions of the green on any given day. After figuring this into the equation, I am usually able to give Tom an extremely precise yardage estimate, always within a yard. As Tom knows exactly how far he can hit each iron, having accurate yardage allows him to home in on the hole, greatly enhancing our chances at birdie.

Though the greenskeeper on your home course won't change pin placements on a daily basis, he or she will change them at least once per week to allow heavily trafficked areas on the green to recover and to make the game more challenging.

This makes it essential for you to know the general dimensions of each green. Though you won't be given a pin sheet at the start of each round, you can keep a few 3" × 5" cards in your bag that show basic green shapes and dimensions in yards. Draw the green, then draw in some sample pin locations. Then give the distances of those pin coordinates from the center of each green. Measuring how far back, front, left, or right they are from the center will allow you to dial your approach shots in properly. Learn the dimensions of each green by pacing them off quickly, after you and your partners have all putted out (unless you have a group pressing you from behind).

Knowing precise green dimensions will also teach you exactly how much club you will need to put a ball onto the green or keep it from running off the back. For instance, if you know that you are 150 yards from the center of a green (a perfect 6-iron for you), and the front of the green is 142 yards from you, you can be guaranteed that a well-hit 7-iron will be enough club to make it on. Likewise, if the back of the green is 164 yards from you, you will know that a 5-iron will be the most club you could possibly keep on the green. Pin placement and wind conditions will then dictate exactly which club you will use.

Tee Boxes

Don't ignore the design of each hole's tee box. Some sneaky course designers purposely aim tee boxes slightly away from the ideal direction your ball should take. Line up your tee shots just as you always would, disregarding how the tee box is situated.

Use a portion of the tee box that is best suited to the type of shot you intend to hit. For instance, if you intend to fade the ball, it's usually best to set up on the far-right side. A draw, on the other hand, normally calls for setting up on the left side. What is more important, however, is using a portion of the tee box that is relatively level and free of visual distractions. Your tee shot is the only time you are allowed to build a perfect lie; don't tee the ball up above or below your feet or position it within a portion of the tee box that has lots of divots or loose impediments that could affect your footing or cause a visual distraction.

Into Thin Air

The altitude of your course can have a profound effect on ball flight. A course built at (or below) sea level will afford you the least amount of carry. Courses built at higher altitudes (such as in Colorado) will add substantial distance to your shots, often as much as ten to twenty percent in some cases. Most golfers experience this while playing rounds on vacation, on courses with very different altitudes than their home courses. When Tom and I compete at high altitude, we always take care to put in a good amount of time on the practice range to learn exactly how much farther each club is traveling. You should do the same to avoid embarrassment and difficult recovery shots that have flown ten or twenty yards past the green, often into the next tee box.

Do not forget about temperature and humidity, two factors that can profoundly affect ball flight and distance. Playing a course in the warmth of summer, with temperatures up around seventy-five or eighty degrees, will assure you maximum distance. Playing that same course in February, when temperatures are down in the forty-five- to fifty-degree range, will reduce the distance of your shots by a good ten to fifteen percent. A 7-iron approach shot in July often turns into a 6-iron in February. Humidity will affect ball flight as well; play a round during a misty, cool, or foggy morning, and you will experience a decrease in distance. Play that same course on a dry, sunny day and distances will increase.

In addition, your shots will carry farther in the dry desert air than under more humid conditions. A 6-iron hit in Phoenix will travel farther than the same shot in Detroit. Paying attention to these factors could mean the difference between sticking a green or landing your errant ball in big trouble.

Yardage Books

Nothing is more important to a caddie's well-being (and job security) than an accurate yardage book. I simply could not do my job without first being given an accurate yardage book for each tournament course Tom and I compete on. Knowing precise hole design as well as distances to hazards, prominent landmarks, greens, and other important course features allows me to give Tom the ability to relax and hit his shot, knowing that the ball (if hit properly) will come to rest close to the desired landing position. Having a good yardage book allows you to play "position" golf instead of the "swing and pray" game that most amateurs play.

The pros depend on yardage books completely these days, unlike in years past. Ben Hogan, for example, used to scoff at players who tried to use accurate yardage measurements to determine club selection. Jack Nicklaus was, I believe, one of the first big-name pros to pace off his distances on a regular basis (and look what it did for his game).

Most Tour players (Tom included) own and use laser range finders. Though not allowed to use them during competition, we can and do make use of them during practice rounds on Monday, Tuesday, or Wednesday, especially on courses we are not too familiar with. With it, I am able to get exact yardages for all visible sprinkler heads, hazards, and prominent objects on the course, such as trees, large rock formations, or even swales or horrendous patches of rough. Additionally, use the laser range finder at your local driving range to verify the yardages of the targets provided. Though clearly marked, these target signs can often be off by as much as five or ten yards.

If you can afford one, by all means get a range finder. You can even share the price with a friend, as the device needn't be used every time you play, but only on new courses.

Having an accurate yardage book for your home course allows you to plan your campaign, so to speak, much in the same way a general plans an attack on enemy soil. It is a map of the battlefield, complete with accurate information about troop strengths, defense strategies, minefields, enemy strongholds, inaccessible areas, and chinks in the enemy's armor, namely ideal landing spots for your ball. In fact, that's what Tom and I do out there; we play an intricate war game against an ingenious course designer and against good old Mother Nature. A yardage book is the equivalent to military intelligence information gathered by your side's spies, giving you an inside glimpse into your opponent's defenses and strategies. If you know where your opponent's troops, booby traps, and vulnerabilities are located, you stand a good chance of breaking through and scoring a direct hit on the prize, namely the hole. Combined with daily pin location sheets given to us each day of a tournament, Tom and I have ample information to do battle, and we often win.

If a yardage book for your home course exists, by all means buy one immediately. Then, over a period of days, study it. Go over each hole carefully and take note of all pertinent features, including out-of-bounds, water, heavy rough, trees, traps, distances, unique designs (such as doglegs or changes in elevation), green shape, dimensions and slope, and even tee box locations. If you have played the course before, you can compare the information in the book to your own course memories. Remember that trap? Or that infernal grove of aspens? Having it all in front of you lends a real sense of clarity; you can see each hole in its entirety and begin to understand what the course designer had in mind when laying out each hole. He or she creates difficulties and opportunities on every shot. Having the yardage book in your hands gives you the chance to see the entire forest, so to speak, rather than each darned tree.

Study carefully the yardages from tees to fairway landing areas, and from landing areas to greens. By doing so, you will be able to decide in advance on general club selection (though this will always need to be ultimately decided upon on the course, once factors such as wind, lie, temperature, and greens speed are determined). You will be able to see clearly why, for instance, your tee shots on that dogleg par-4 hole have almost always ended up in the right rough. Without knowing precisely at what yardage the turn of the hole begins, you have unknowingly been driving the ball slightly past the elbow and running it off the fairway. The yardage book will show you distance to this spot and convince you to use a 3-wood or a 2-iron off the tee instead, or to use a draw to turn the corner nicely, keeping the ball in the fairway.

Unfortunately, many courses do not have a yardage book available to its players. Creating one can be a rather costly endeavor; many course managers simply forgo the expense and instead produce a glorified scorecard, showing each hole's basic design but often ignoring yardages to specific hazards or key landing areas. Normally these scorecards only provide total yardage for each hole as well as a small schematic, usually not large enough to show important details. Though very helpful, these brief "course summaries" would never do for a Tour player and shouldn't for you, either.

Michael Carrick and Steve Duno

Making Your Own Yardage Book

If no yardage book exists for your course, you should make one. Utilizing the course's available scorecard information in combination with your own personal playing experiences should allow you to piece together a very usable and helpful record that includes all necessary data. Each hole's basic design can be sketched onto the back of a 3" × 5" note card and should include penciled-in yardages to every important point, such as fairway bunkers, water hazards, and ideal landing areas. These yardages can be easily measured by using a laser range finder or by using the old-fashioned method of pacing it off. Don't measure distances from the tee all the way to the green (except on par-3s); instead, measure distances to landing areas, then distances from those areas to the front of the green. In doing so, you will give yourself a good feel for what club will be needed on each shot. Be sure to show distances to points of reference on the course, such as sprinkler heads, bushes, trees, and dogleg elbows, so that you can apply the yardage statistics properly when on the course. Make sure to include green shape, depth, and breadth as well as location of primary and secondary rough. In addition, try using arrows to show the general direction of the grain on the greens. I do this for all Bermuda greens we play on; it helps us to remember direction and speed. The grain on bent grass greens doesn't affect putts nearly as much, so I rarely take note of it.

Try using colored pencils on your homemade yardage book.

The added contrast and color will make the diagram more user-friendly.

In addition, don't forget to pencil in the width of landing areas for each par-4 or par-5 fairway. Knowing where the widest and most narrow areas are can really help in the decision-making process. For instance, if you normally hit a driver 260 yards, but find that the fairway is only 25 yards wide at that distance out, you might want to throttle back to a 3-wood or 2-iron, just to play it safe.

On the lined side of the 3" × 5" card, write down any pertinent information you feel you need, such as:

- What type of tee shot is needed (draw, fade, low, or high)
- Ideal landing area
- Ideal approach shot
- Slopes of the fairways and the greens
- Ideal clubs to use
- Prevailing winds on that hole
- Strategic thoughts, such as "keep it left" or "below the hole"
- Speed of that hole's green
- Special info, such as "third green extra firm" or "fifth hole plays shorter than yardage"

You can even write down a positive, happy thought, such as "birdied it last spring" or "won twenty from Joe on this hole last summer." Just make sure that you don't put down more information than can be absorbed in a quick glance, as you will be using the card while waiting for your turn on the tee.

Once you have a card for each hole, simply staple or clip them together and keep them in your bag. Studying them the night before a round will give you a real head start on your opponent and on the course itself. You can make one of these homemade yardage books for each of the three or four courses you most regularly play.

Playing in the Morning

Most courses take a fair amount of abuse from players over the course of a day. By the afternoon, spike and ball marks, divots, and ejected sand often pepper every fairway or green. Also, wind and rain often become more pronounced later in the day. If you are unlucky enough to play later in the day, you will need to deal with all of these problems, which often results in a score much higher than what is normal for you.

An easy solution is to simply get an early tee time. By doing so, you won't have to putt through spike marks or hit out of fresh divots. The wind probably won't be as strong, and any rain in the forecast might not yet be falling. Also, morning dew on the greens will slow your putts down a bit, making lagging a bit easier (though the same dew might result in slightly shorter drives due to less run). All in all, morning rounds offer more favorable conditions, particularly on busy public courses. Set that alarm a few hours earlier than normal and give it a try.

On Playing a Wet Course

Most amateurs hate playing in the rain or when the course is wet and soft. The pros, however, love damp conditions for one important reason, summed up by two words: *low scores*. When a course is wet, the fairways and greens are easier to hold. Balls don't tend to run off into the rough or through the green as often. Long irons into a small green become much less risky, and "flyer lies" become less significant. A wet, soft course provides the pros with the chance to play target practice all day; where a ball lands is pretty much where it will end up. Balls become darts, so to speak. The only negative aspect is, of course, keeping your grips and glove dry enough to prevent slippage, which can cause errant shots or flying clubs. Just be sure to have a number of clean, dry towels with you to wipe down your grips and a good supply of gloves, which may need changing several times during the round. Also, try keeping your glove wrapped around one of the spokes of your opened umbrella to protect it from the rain.

Basic Pre-shot Routines and Address Positions Used by the Pros

As stated earlier, golf, perhaps more than any other, is a game of rituals, and not without good reason. Overanalyzing, one of the greatest enemies of any golfer, can often become rampant inside our brains, due mainly to stage fright and a fear of failure. Nothing is more annoying or embarrassing than a failed shot, especially in front of others. The desire to avoid this causes many golfers to fill their minds with dozens of swing thoughts each time they step up to a shot, resulting in brain overload and a lousy shot. Ritual, or a repeatable, preordained series of ceremonial acts, can help prevent this. In golf, the pre-shot routine serves this purpose well. Every good golfer has a routine he or she goes through before each shot to create the right mindset, switch on muscle memory, and engage subconscious thoughts needed to swing the club properly. An effective pre-shot routine clears the mind of negative thoughts and allows the body to do its thing smoothly and effectively.

To succeed on the course, you need to develop a well thought-out pre-shot routine, just like the pros. But just what does that entail? Let me take you through an example that Tom and I might encounter during a tournament. Tom has hit his tee shot on a dogleg-right par-4, a hole that calls for a soft fade. Unfortunately his ball does not fade and ends up in light rough on the left side of the fairway, about 140 yards from the pin, which on this day is located in the back-right section of the long, thin, unprotected green.

Tom's pre-shot routine begins as we are walking up to his ball. The first step is a quick analysis of the lie and the type of shot needed. The ball has nestled down a bit, meaning that some grass will get in between the ball and the club head, reducing green-holding spin and causing the ball to fly a bit farther than usual. Normally an 8-iron, Tom decides to hit 9-iron, counting on the flyer lie. As the pin is tucked in back-right, he decides to hit a soft fade, insurance against the ball scooting through the green into the back bunker.

The analysis over, Tom goes into the ritualistic, non-thinking part of his pre-shot routine. First, he stands behind the ball and decides on the proper aim. As many Tour players do, he chooses a spot a few feet in front of the ball that is in line with the pin, and then aims the club head directly down this path. Then, to induce a slight fade, he sets up with his feet and shoulders ever so slightly open, a position that will encourage a subtle out-to-in swing. Tom then takes one practice swing, waggles the club a few times, peddles his weight back and forth quickly from foot to foot, looks at the target quickly, then lets it go.

Except for variations in the type of shot, that is the same routine Tom has used for years. Other players have slightly different ingredients; Justin Leonard and Karrie Webb, for instance, always include a precise quarter-swing waggle before every shot. Nicklaus has his patented head tilt right before he unloads. Whatever the unique ingredient, every player always does the same thing before a shot.

You should ingrain your own pre-shot routine, just as the

pros do. After analyzing your shot situation (covered completely in a later section of this book), begin your aiming procedure. Choosing a spot on line with the hole a few feet in front of your ball works well; stand behind the ball and see the line clearly, perhaps even imagining a bright yellow line leading from your ball to the pin (or landing area). Then, after a few practice swings, step up to the ball, place the club head along your imagined line, and take your stance, which could be open, closed, or neutral, depending on the type of shot you intend to hit. At this point, many players waggle the club head, as a way to loosen up the muscles. If you do so, fine; just do it every time. Some players, Tom Kite and Raymond Floyd, for example, shift their weight back and forth from foot to foot before swinging. Others have a head tilt, or a quick knee bend. Whatever you get into the habit of doing, *try to do it every time*. It will become part of your ingrained ritual and will help relax your mind and body in preparation for the swing. Keep it simple and repeatable.

Tour professionals never change their pre-shot routines, but they often adjust their address positions in order to hit a specific type of shot. Let me go over the basic types of shots and what address position adjustment you will need to make in order to hit them properly.

The Mythical Straight Shot

First, let me say that, except for Fred Funk, players rarely hit a dead straight golf shot. Almost everyone has a natural inclina-

The Straight Shot: Your feet, hips, shoulders,
and club face should all be parallel.

tion toward either a fade or a draw. Trevino and Nicklaus, for
example, are natural faders, whereas Kite and Lehman normally draw the ball. When they step up to the tee, however,
they aren't necessarily trying to hit to either side; it just occurs
naturally, and they take advantage of it. Most shots, however,
particularly off the tee, often do call for a definite fade or draw,
depending on which way the fairway turns or banks, what side
of the fairway sets up best for the approach shot, or how much
distance you need off the tee. Depending on the conditions,

then, a Tour player will intentionally hit a fade or draw, with varying levels of success.

If the player's natural shot shape is all that is needed (say, for instance, on a relatively straight-on fairway), the player will address the ball with a neutral stance, with feet parallel to the line of the shot. The club head is set up "square," positioned exactly perpendicular to the desired line of flight. The ball position is often unique to the player, but it is generally played slightly closer to the leading foot by faders. This address position will produce the closest thing to a straight shot possible for most players, provided the swing path used delivers the club head to the ball in a perfectly square manner, neither from the inside or the outside. On this shot, there is definitely a "release" of the club head, meaning that the trailing hand turns over the leading hand in a natural, unforced manner, dictated by centrifugal force.

The Draw

A draw is certainly a very handy shot to have in your arsenal, particularly if:

- A fairway doglegs to the left
- An approach shot calls for the ball to be positioned in the left portion of the fairway
- The fairway slopes from left to right
- The green is protected on the left side (or right, for a left-handed golfer) by a hazard

The Draw: Align your body to the right and
aim the club face at the target.

- A particularly long amount of roll is required
- A tree prevents you from hitting a straight shot or a
  fade

Whatever the reason, a pro often needs to pull a draw out of
his or her bag and can usually do so quite handily. It is done
by first determining the proper line of the shot, then aiming the
club head slightly to the right of it (or to the left, for a lefty) by
a few degrees in a "closed" position. Then, the ball is addressed

with the trailing foot pulled back a few inches so that the line of the player's feet (and shoulders) is aimed a few degrees to the right (or left, for a lefty) of the line to the pin.

Some players will move the ball back an inch or so in the stance to insure that the club head will contact the ball while it is still on an inside track. Then the player simply takes his or her normal swing, with perhaps a bit more of a feeling of release than with the straight shot. If a Tour player needs to hit a stronger draw, he or she usually tries to exaggerate that feel of release, with the trailing hand really turning over the leading hand smartly. On most draw shots, though, this exaggerated release is not used, as it can often be hard to modulate. The basic draw, then, is easier to create by simple adjustments to the address position.

The Fade

The fade is an important shot to be able to execute, particularly if:

- The fairway doglegs to the right
- An approach shot calls for the ball to be positioned on the right side of the fairway
- The fairway slopes from right to left
- The green is protected on the right side (or the left side, for a lefty) by a hazard
- A higher-flying, soft-landing shot with less roll is needed

The Fade: Align your body to the left and the
club face at the target.

- A tree is preventing you from making a straight shot
  or a draw

Most amateurs' natural shot is a fade (or a dreaded slice).
Because of this, most instinctively know how to reproduce one,
though not necessarily with the same amount of control and
precision as can a Tour pro. When needed, Tom and other pros
can dial in a fade by first determining the proper line to the pin,

Michael Carrick and Steve Duno

then aiming the club head slightly to the right of that line, in an "open" position. Then the ball is addressed with a slightly open stance, with the right foot moved forward an inch or so. Some players will also move the ball up an inch in their stances to insure that the club head will contact the ball on a slightly out-to-in track. Then a normal swing is taken, with a definite feeling of holding back slightly on the release, keeping the club head open somewhat through the follow-through. If a player needs to create a more pronounced fade (read "slice"), he or she will simply set up with a more open stance and take a more pronounced out-to-in swing, with a definite feeling of cutting across the ball.

The High Shot

Sometimes a player needs to hit a higher, softer shot than normal, for a number of reasons. For example, Tom might have an 8-iron approach shot to a pin that is only fifteen feet onto a slick green, protected in front by a bunker. The ball must land softly and not run. Or, a tree might be directly in front of his ball, preventing a normal 8-iron shot due to insufficient clearance. Whatever the reason, sometimes a player just needs to get a bit more height on a shot in order to stay in the hunt.

Getting the ball up higher than normal isn't too hard to do. Play the ball about an inch closer to your lead foot, open the club head and your stance slightly, and take a smooth, sweeping swing, avoiding too steep of an approach. The ball should pop up nice and high, with the altitude of one shorter club. You might even need to take one extra club to allow for the lost distance, though doing so depends entirely on the conditions present, including the wind, lie, and green shape, slope, and speed.

The High Shot: Play the ball up in your stance and open your stance slightly. Aim the club face at the target and do not let your hands get ahead of the ball.

The Low Shot

Tom is a great wind player. He craves blustery conditions because it always helps "cull the herd," so to speak; less experienced players often go way over par and miss the cut, giving veterans a clear shot at the win. I have watched him hit low screamers under the wind in countless tournaments, particularly ones in the United Kingdom, Florida, and Texas, where conditions are often quite gusty. Being able to do so is a valuable skill that all good golfers possess; by mastering the low shot, you will be able to insure that your shots will not be at the total mercy of the winds.

Say, for instance, you have a 150-yard approach shot to a smallish green, directly into a 30-mph wind. Your regular 7-iron shot will never make it, as the wind will grab it and balloon it up. The harder you swing at it, the higher it will go, due to the extra spin. This ballooning effect will scrub at least 10 or 20 yards off the shot. To overcome this, consider going to a 5- or 6-iron, then gripping down on the club an inch or two. This will guarantee a lower trajectory, but with the same distance as a 7-iron. Next, play the ball back at least an inch from its normal position, get your hands well ahead of the ball, and take a steeper than normal, easy, three-quarter swing, with a lower follow-through, keeping your hands ahead of the ball throughout the swing. You may even want to take a slightly open stance to allow for the club head contacting the ball more from the inside due to the ball being moved back in the stance. Without correcting for this with a more open stance, the ball may end

The Low Shot: Play the ball back in your stance
and position your hands ahead of the ball.
Also, open your stance slightly.

up pushed right. Expect the ball to come out low, with less carry
and more roll.

The Decision-Making Process:
How To Choose the Right Shot

All Tour players are capable of hitting a multitude of different shots, according to what is needed at the time. Some situations call for a high, soft ball flight, while others necessitate a

low, boring shot. Often a fade (or easy right turn for a right-handed player) is needed, though other times a draw (easy turn to the left for a right-handed player) is the ticket. It all depends on course design and conditions present at the time of the shot. Because of experience and countless hours of practice, a pro can quickly decide on what shot to use, often before they even arrive at the ball. The ease at which they make their strategic choices is what makes them so successful at their craft.

The first variable you must consider when deciding upon what type of shot to hit is the distance from your target, be it the pin or the ideal landing spot in the fairway. Being able to determine the exact yardage to the target is crucial to a successful shot, and it is one of the factors that separates pros from amateurs. Tom and I can estimate to within a yard exactly how far his ball is from the target, every time, because we have an accurate yardage book, a pin sheet, and good knowledge of the course we are playing on. In addition, Tom and I know exactly how far he can hit each club in his bag. Amateurs usually walk up to the ball, make a halfhearted attempt at locating a 150-yard marker stick or a sprinkler head with the marked yardage, then choose a club and swing away. They usually do not know how far they can reliably hit each club. So, armed with all of this misinformation, the amateur player's chances of hitting the target are slim to none.

The very first thing you should do to improve your chances of hitting your target is to go to your local practice range (or better yet, a large field where you can pace off exact distances or use a laser range finder) and find out just how far you can *reliably* hit each club in your bag. That doesn't mean maximum distance under perfect conditions, but rather the average distance. To do so, you need to hit ten shots with each club, throw out the thinned or chunked mis-hits, and take the average of the remaining shot distances. Some will be hit flush, while others will be hit toward the toe or heel, just as when on the course. The resulting distance figure will be more representative of what you can expect under pressure situations. So instead of thinking that you hit your 7-iron 150 yards, you probably hit it a *reliable* 145. That is the figure you should take onto the course with you.

Next, you need to be able to determine how far you are from your target in order to choose the proper club. Doing so will be made much easier if you have a yardage book (or have made your own, as described earlier). Knowing exact distances to key points on each hole will allow you to determine precisely how far your target is, as well as the hazards to avoid. For example, as Tom approaches his tee shot and readies himself for the approach, I am calculating exactly how far we have to the front of the green, the pin, and the back of the green, as well as distances to any hazard that might be menacing. I do so by locating a reliable yardage marker (usually a sprinkler head), then pacing off the distance from it to Tom's ball. Then I factor in the yardages I have on my pin sheet and give Tom the exact number. The success of the shot becomes largely one of proper execution, without any added guesswork.

When on the tee, knowing the exact distance to fairway bunkers, water, trees, or any other undesirable landing area will allow you to avoid them nicely. For example, if Tom knows that a cluster of fairway bunkers lies in wait 265 yards out and slightly left, he might decide to drop down to a 3-wood or a long iron. In doing so, he takes the bunkers completely out of the equation. There is no need to worry about a recovery shot from one of the traps. And reducing worry on the course is one strategic key to winning. Tiger Woods certainly wouldn't worry about those fairway bunkers either, because he can hit his driver a reliable 300 yards, every time, right over them. Whether you know you can lay up or fly the hazard, choose one and go with it. If that hazard is only a few yards within the range of a particular club, either drop down or move up a club to eliminate the hazard from your mind. By doing so, you are "playing the percentages" and reducing the chances of bogey or worse.

The next important factor in choosing the right type of shot is the lie of the ball. How the ball sits on the course can vary tremendously, from the perfect lie of a tee shot (sitting up nicely on its wooden peg) to being buried in a bunker or knee-high wild grass. Let's go through the basic lies and what type of shot you can expect to be able to hit out of each. Bear in mind that the lie can vary infinitely, according to the exact conditions of that course on that day.

The Tee Shot

This is an ideal lie because you are allowed to set the ball height wherever you want it. Besides teeing it up high for a driver (allowing a slightly upward approach angle to the ball), the humble tee allows you to hit ideal iron shots as well, by teeing your ball just high enough to mimic a fluffy lie, with about a quarter-inch of space beneath the ball. Most pros use a tee on the first shot, even par-3s, because of this reason. The height of the ball off a tee does not eliminate spin, however (as with a fluffy lie), because no grass ever comes between the ball and club head. Therefore, a teed-up 6-iron shot will hold a green better than one of similar distance from light rough.

Always tee your ball up when you can. Just remember to keep your iron shots teed low, and never as high as with a driver or even a fairway wood.

To hit a high tee shot with your driver, tee your ball up nice and high, especially if you have a deep-faced titanium driver. Make sure that at least half of the ball is above the top of the driver face. Also, play the ball about a half-inch farther up in your stance than normal to guarantee that the club head makes contact on an upward arc. Choose a higher shot like this when you need maximum carry due to a rain-softened fairway, if hitting with the wind, or just when you need that extra ten yards. Avoid this type of high tee shot on a windy day, as the added height of the ball will put it at the mercy of the elements, resulting in a fairway miss or worse. Also, expect this higher shot to fade and not run as far as a normal tee shot.

Tee it up lower if the winds are howling into your face or from the side. A low tee shot will be affected less by the wind, and it will tend to roll more once it hits the fairway. Also hit the lower shot if the fairways are dry and hard; the lower trajectory will often encourage the ball to scoot an extra forty or fifty yards, making your approach shot easier. Do this only if no fairway bunkers, dramatic drop-offs, or other hazards are in the way.

To hit your driver low, tee the ball up so that the top of it is only a quarter-inch or so above the top of your driver face. Also, play the ball about half an inch back from its normal position to encourage a flatter angle of attack.

The Tight Fairway Lie

Generally the most preferred lie on the course, the tight, clean lie of a ball on the fairway allows Tour pros to generate maximum spin, as no grass gets in between the club head and ball. With a tight fairway lie, the ball position should not be too far forward in the stance, to prevent thinning or chunking a shot. A precise swing will make contact with the ball just before the bottom of the swing arc, insuring proper elevation on the shot. All pros want to get into the fairway on their first shots in order to obtain this preferred lie.

The "Fluffy" Lie

When you miss the fairway, often the ball will end up in the secondary cut of rough, normally no longer than half an inch in length. Often the most confidence-inspiring lie for amateurs due to the ball being slightly elevated (as on a tee), pros can have some trouble with a fluffy lie, as some grass will end up coming in between the ball and club head, reducing spin and creating a slight "flyer lie," in which the ball often travels farther than normal and does not check up as well on the green.

With a fluffy lie, play the ball about an inch farther back in your stance to insure a slightly steeper swing, minimizing the chance of grass getting in between the club head and ball. Consider landing the ball at least ten yards shorter than if you were hitting from the fairway, allowing for more roll. This may mean hitting one less club or gripping down on the normal club choice. Avoid slowing down your swing, as this could cause deceleration through the ball and a resulting mis-hit.

The "Hardpan" Lie

Sometimes your ball will end up on bare turf or on a patch of packed-down dirt. At first intimidating, this type of lie needn't be feared. Pros know that to successfully hit from hardpan, you need to insure that the club head makes contact with the ball first. If it doesn't, it will bounce up and catch the ball at the equator, causing an embarrassing, thinned shot that never gets more than a few feet off the ground.

To effectively hit off of hardpan, simply move the ball back in your stance at least two inches and make a steeper swing. Consider opening your stance slightly as well.

Heavy Rough

Here is where trouble can start, for pros and amateurs alike. When the ball is sitting down in rough longer than half an inch, the chances of getting enough club head on the ball are slim. Almost certainly, the ball will not come out with enough velocity to carry it very far. Also, if the rough is deep enough, the hosel of your iron may get caught by the high grass, causing the blade to close. This will send your ball off to the left, possibly into more trouble.

Don't try to be a hero in the deep stuff. Just get the ball out and back into the fairway. If you can advance it also, so much the better. Often, though, you might have to pitch out laterally just to find some short grass. Take a lofted club, open the blade up slightly to allow for the hosel getting caught, and take a smooth swing. Consider tightening your grip just a bit to maintain the club head angle through the thick grass.

Bermuda rough is normally harder to hit out of than bent rough, as the ball always tends to sink down to the bottom. Plus, Bermuda rough is more wiry than bent, making it harder to get the club through. If playing out of Bermuda rough, don't attempt any heroics unless absolutely necessary!

Divots

You have hit what appears to be a perfect tee shot, landing the ball in the ideal part of the fairway for an easy approach. Upon arriving at the ball, however, you find it sitting in someone's old divot mark. What is the problem here?

Hitting out of a divot can be very difficult for a number of reasons. First, the ball is lying on dirt, not turf, making contact with the ball first essential. Second, the ball may be sitting low in the front part of the divot, causing it to sit tightly against a low wall of turf. This can cause mis-hits or severely short shots because the ball is, in effect, below ground level. Third, many old divots are filled in with sand; if you are unlucky enough to find your ball in one of these, you will have, in effect, a bunker shot in miniature, requiring you to pick the ball off cleanly. Payne Stewart arguably lost the 1998 U.S. Open to Lee Janzen because of a ruined approach shot from a sand-filled divot.

To hit out of a divot, play the ball back in your stance about an inch or so and get your hands well ahead of the ball to promote a steep angle of attack. Use a more lofted club as well, to make up for the de-lofting of the club. Then just concentrate on making contact with the ball first.

Sand

Perhaps the widest discrepancy between the game's amateurs and Tour players can be seen inside the bunker. Average players fear the sand; pros don't mind it at all. The problem with the lie of a ball on sand is that sand is a fluid substance that absorbs energy and does not allow a player to hit out of it with a normal pitch or chip technique. The difference between success and failure out of the sand boils down to practice, practice, and more practice, something many weekend golfers do not do because of two reasons: most public courses do not have practice bunkers available, and most amateurs prefer to practice their long games rather than their short games.

The lie of a ball in a fairway bunker is often the same as the lie of a ball in a greenside bunker, though a ball hit into a greenside bunker can more often become buried due to the steeper angle of entry the ball usually takes, a result of a more lofted club used for the approach shot. Balls that end up in a fairway bunker usually got there off the face of a driver or long iron, which impart a shallow trajectory to the ball, almost insuring some minimal "run" in the bunker, reducing the chance of a ball plugging.

Hitting out of a fairway bunker requires the player to make contact with the ball first, much in the same way as off of hardpan. However, the shot is less forgiving. Hit a ball off of a hardpan lie a bit fat and you will still advance the ball a good distance, as the club head will bounce into the equator of the ball and create a low bullet that won't get more than a few feet off the ground. Hit it fat out of a fairway bunker, however, and the ball might not go ten feet. So, contact with the ball first is paramount. To do so, set up as if you were hitting off of hardpan, with the ball slightly back in your stance, and make a steeper swing. Also, try opening your stance a bit and keep your lower body steady, with little weight shift. Make sure to use plenty of loft, especially if the lip of the bunker is high. If the lip is low, you may be able to use a lofted fairway wood; avoid using any iron longer than a 5-iron, though, unless you have perfected the shot.

Hitting out of a greenside bunker is easy once you get the hang of it. If the ball is sitting up nicely, just position the ball up in your stance (about off your leading heel), open up your sand wedge blade and your stance, and make a smooth swing, aiming to make contact with the sand about two inches behind the ball. Be sure to make a full follow-through and really try for a feeling of "splashing" through the sand. Also try to limit your lower body movement, make sure to dig into the sand with your feet, and grip down on the club about two inches to compensate for this. And practice, practice, practice.

If you have a buried lie in the sand, play the ball closer to the middle of your stance, aim your club head straight down your intended line (instead of wide open), and make a steeper swing, punching down into the sand about an inch or so behind the ball. The ball should pop out and run quite a ways, so allow for that. Unlike the regular splash shot, this "explosion" shot will have little if any follow-through.

Cart Path

Hitting your ball off of a cart path luckily will not be a common experience, as you do receive a free drop onto more friendly turf. However, sometimes that free drop will place your ball behind a tree or some other obstruction that does not allow a clear shot to the green. Under these conditions, you may need to hit off the cart path. To make this shot, simply hit the ball as you would off of hardpan, making contact with the ball first. Try to make a shallower swing, and keep your lower body out of the equation. And do not take a divot!

Pine Needles or Leaves

Necessitating the same basic technique as hitting off of hardpan, the problem with pine needles or leaves comes during your approach and set-up to the ball. As you know, if your ball moves while addressed, you incur a penalty. To avoid this, the pros never ground their clubs on shots off of pine needles or leaves, which can often interlock together and cause a ball to move if a club is grounded as far as six or eight inches away. Treat this shot as you would one from a hazard, where you are prohibited from grounding your club. Take a steeper swing, and make sure to make contact with the ball first.

Water

What can I say? Few shots out of the water are successfully pulled off, even by the pros. First, water refracts light and prevents you from discerning the true position of your ball, preventing clean contact. Second, water will decelerate the club head and cause major deflection of the blade. It is normally a lose-lose situation and one calling for a drop.

However, if the ball is sitting up high in water, with only a quarter-inch of ball below the surface, you may be able to hit it out. To do so, first put on your rain gear, take off your shoes and socks, then set up with the ball back in your stance. Keeping your lower body still, make a steep, three-quarter swing into the back of the ball, making sure to catch the ball first. With some luck, the ball should pop out. My advice: try this only if your entire life savings is on the table!

General Shot Strategy Guidelines

The next issue to think about once you have taken the lie of the ball into consideration is: where do you want to hit the ball? For all Tour players, this issue of position is the key decision for every shot. Position is everything. Most amateurs just hit the ball and hope for the best, a non-strategy that results in huge scores and unpleasant experiences. Amateurs also think that distance and position are synonymous, but they are not. Though distance off of the tee is very helpful to scoring, accuracy and proper placement are more crucial. I would rather have a 175-yard shot into the green from a tight fairway lie than a 120-yard shot from the deep woods any day. Wouldn't you? Yes, Woods or Duval hit wedge approach shots all day long, but, frankly, we are not them. We need to think about playing the best we can within our own games. You may not be able to hit 300-yard drives, but you can hit the proper part of the fairway.

Let's discuss effective shot strategies off of the tee, from the fairway, and around the greens. First, you must have a clear understanding of the conditions present before ever making a shot. Your choice of shot should be determined largely by the strength and direction of the wind, the lie, the overall weather pattern (including temperature, amount of precipitation, and so on), the altitude, and elevation change. For instance:

- Hitting into a 20-mph wind will necessitate a much lower trajectory to avoid having the wind wreak havoc on the flight of the ball.
- Hitting out of a flyer lie means allowing for extra carry and run.
- Hitting any shot at an altitude of 5,000 feet means allowing for at least ten percent more carry.
- Hitting a shot in cold weather conditions means less carry.
- Hitting a shot on a wet course means less roll.

These and other conditions present must be factored into your decision-making process before a swing is ever made. Failing to do so will result in a loss of accuracy and a more frequent need for heroic recovery shots.

Next, you must know what your target is. Even on a tee shot, always choose a target and concentrate on landing your ball right on top of it. If it is a tee shot, choose a spot in the fairway. If a par-3, choose either the pin or a spot on a fat, level portion of the green. Do not just get up there and swing away without aiming at a precise spot! Make sure that target spot leaves you with the best possible angle into the green. For instance, if the pin is back left, generally you would want to be making your approach shot from the right side of the fairway.

Try to know the exact yardage to your target. Even an amateur on his or her home course can calculate this if a course-supplied (or homemade) yardage book exists. By knowing this (and the precise distances that you can hit each club), you take much of the guesswork out of the equation.

Always develop and utilize an ingrained pre-shot routine before every shot you take. Doing so will clear your mind of negative thoughts, improve focus, and help engage muscle memory.

Become aware of the hazards present on each shot in order to help determine the ideal target. Try ranking the hazards according to the severity of penalty, as well as difficulty in getting out. Generally, rank hazards in the following order:

1. Out-of-bounds
2. Water
3. High grass or rocks
4. Trees
5. Rough
6. Sand
7. Downhill or sidehill lie

By knowing exactly where the hazards are and by knowing the dangers of each, you will be able to decide on the best target and the safest shot shape. For instance, if out-of-bounds runs along the entire left side of a hole, you know to favor the right side of a fairway. This may call for a fade that is aimed toward the middle of the fairway. If the ball does fade, it will end up right of center. If the ball fails to fade, it will still avoid out-of-bounds and land somewhere in the center of the fairway. A good philosophy might be to decide on where the best place to miss a shot might be.

Always try to land your ball in a relatively flat section of fairway, even if it means having a slightly longer approach shot into the pin. Remember, a flat lie is always preferable to a downhill or sidehill lie and usually preferable to an uphill lie as well.

If you are ever in doubt about which club to hit, *go with more club*. If I had to choose the biggest error made by amateurs during a pro-am, it would have to be under-clubbing, then not being able to get the ball up and down from wherever it ended up. Statistically, more trouble exists in front of, or to the sides of, a green than in back. So even if you overshoot the green, odds are that your recovery will be easier. Remember, *play the percentages*.

Know what shape shot best fits the situation. If hitting a tee shot on a severe dogleg right, for instance, common sense says to play a fade. Or, if making an approach shot to a green with its pin tucked far left and back, a draw may be in order.

If you are not yet able to shape your shots, then be aware of whatever the natural curve of your shot is, and then apply it as best you can to the situation. If you fade every shot, a dogleg right will be no problem. If the hole is a dogleg left, however, a fader of the ball will need to make sure that a target area exists for his or her shot. This may mean throttling back a club or two just to keep the ball in the fairway. The same goes for a natural draw; try to fit it into the space given, making sure to club up or down accordingly. Whatever you do, *keep it in the fairway*.

Have the best short game possible, as most amateurs will not get onto the green in regulation. Reliably getting up and down from just off the green requires a great pitching and chipping game that can regularly put the ball within five feet of the pin, giving the player a good shot at making par. Spend at least half of your practice time chipping, pitching, and putting and try to simulate real conditions while doing so. For example, don't chip ball after ball from the same perfect lie and spot; instead, throw a dozen or so balls down randomly, and hit them from where they lie. That means some from the short fringe, some from light rough, and others from deeper stuff. Vary the distance from the green also. In addition, don't putt ball after ball from the same spot. Putt one from thirty feet, then one from four feet. Putt a few from the fringe. Hit one long, breaking downhill putt, then follow it up with a short, uphill two-footer. By varying your practice in this way, you will learn feel, one of the biggest advantages the pro has over the amateur.

Playing a Par-3

One of the keys to correctly playing a par-3 hole is to think of it as nothing more than an approach shot on a par-4. By doing so, you will relieve much of the pressure felt on the tee. In fact, it is an easier shot because you can choose the lie and position of the ball.

First, size up the pin position and the overall shape and slope of the green. If it is a relatively large, flat green with the pin located near the center, you can feel safe about going for the pin. If the green has lots of slope changes and a pin tucked in behind a hazard (or far left or right, close to trouble), then your strategy must change. Your target then becomes the flattest, widest part of the green that will present you with the flattest putt, or one that is uphill. Avoid like the plague downhill putts, especially ones that break. That is the lesson the pros learn at the Masters each spring; Augusta's fast, undulating greens almost guarantee three-putts, unless your approach shots all land below the hole. During the 1997 Masters, that's just what Tiger did. I don't think he three-putted a single green that week, resulting in a record score and a lapping of the field.

If the depth of the green on a par-3 is very shallow, consider hitting a high fade off the tee instead of a draw. A fade will come in higher and land more softly, with less roll and more spin. Also hit a fade if the target area is located in the back of a green that tails off at a left-to-right angle, relative to the line of the shot. Additionally, hit the trusty fade if the target landing area is located in the front of the green, as you do not want the ball to roll much upon landing. Conversely, hit a draw off the tee if the green is a long one that tails off the left, relative to the line of the shot. Any par-3 green with a target landing area located in the far back will also accept a draw happily, as the ball will roll farther due to a lower trajectory and less backspin.

Of course, the shape of your tee shot on any par-3 will also be affected by any hazards in your way. If a tree limb juts out one hundred yards down the fairway on the left side, for example, you may need to avoid any type of fade shot. Or if a bunker guards the right-front portion of a green, a draw might be a bad choice, as it would require the ball to travel directly over it for a time. If that ball didn't travel exactly as far as you had hoped, it will end up on the beach, threatening your par. In general, choose a shot shape that doesn't require the ball to fly over any portion of a hazard at any time.

On a very long par-3 (over 200 yards), don't be afraid to lay up short of the green, if trying to land the ball on the green is too risky a venture. For instance, on a 225-yard par-3 hole with water on three sides of the green, the better percentage shot for you just might be landing the ball 20 or 30 yards short of the water and pitching it into the pin. If your short game is sharp, this strategy just might be the higher percentage shot. Better to hit a 4- or 5-iron and pitch the ball than to take your chances with a 3- or 5-wood into a well-guarded green.

Playing a Par-4

First, take stock of the conditions, particularly the wind. Check the trees, the clouds, and grass dropped from your hand. Remember that wind at the tee box might be totally different from wind near the landing area in the fairway. If the wind is blowing into your face, hit an extra club or two; generally for every ten mph of wind, you'll need to hit one more club. Attempt a lower ball flight into a strong wind by teeing the ball lower and slightly farther back in your stance. Then make sure you take a smooth swing. If the shot is downwind, use less club, unless there is no threat of overshooting the desired landing area. Hit a nice high shot by teeing high and farther up in your stance. A side wind will require you to compensate with your aim and shot type. For a left-to-right wind, choose your target spot in the fairway, then aim slightly left of it. Or if your draw is good, curve the ball right into that wind, effectively canceling out its effects. For a right-left wind, simply do the opposite. Aim right of your desired landing spot or curve a nice fade right into it. Done properly, the wind and the fade will cancel each other out, and the ball will land exactly where you want it to. This takes lots of practice, so get out onto that practice tee and work on it!

Study the shape of the hole on a par-4 and play to it. Dogleg left? Hit a draw. Dogleg right? Fade it. Straight fairway? Choose the side of the fairway that will set up for the best approach shot and aim for that. Imagine that there is a pin stuck right in the ideal landing spot in the fairway and aim for it, shutting out all negative thoughts. Don't think about where not to hit it; just think about that pin stuck in the fairway.

Know all the hazards and trouble spots on that par-4. Out-of-bounds all along the left side? Avoid it like the plague and hit a fade aimed at the center of the fairway. Fairway bunkers on the right, 200 yards out? Hit a draw, using enough club to fly the bunkers just in case the ball doesn't turn. Or club down to eliminate the bunkers entirely. If you hit a 4-iron a reliable 185 yards, then use it off the tee with absolute confidence. Play the percentage shot, and don't worry about impressing your partners or yourself. Your score after 18, and not your total driving distance, will speak for itself.

Don't always grab your driver on a par-4. If the ideal target area in the fairway is narrow, consider going with a 3-, 4-, or 5-wood, or a long iron, which all afford more accuracy than the driver. Also, if the par-4 is a short one (under 325 yards), always consider hitting a club that will leave you with a full approach shot into the green. Too many amateurs during pro-ams hit driver and leave themselves with an awkward yardage into the green, usually a 40- or 50-yard shot that requires them to throttle back on a sand wedge. This shot is hard enough for a pro, let alone an amateur, because the partial swing required cannot impart green-holding spin to the ball. More often than not, the ball rolls through the green into a bunker or some thick rough, eliminating any shot at par. Usually, try to leave yourself with an 80- to 100-yard approach shot on a short par-4; this will let you hit a full wedge and hold the green. On a 325-yard hole, then, you should choose a club off the tee that you can reliably hit 225 to 240 yards. That may be a 2-iron, 3-wood, or driver, depending on your length. Just don't land your tee shot out at that dreaded 30- to 50-yard distance.

Choose the flattest landing area that will afford you a clear approach shot into the green. Pounding the ball out 280 yards won't help at all if it lands on a severe slope or a bunker.

If the pin is located on the right portion of the green, try landing your tee shot on the left side of the fairway to give you the best angle in. If the pin is located left, land the tee shot on the right side of the fairway. If hazards or severe slopes prevent this, however, just choose the safest fairway target and go for it. Above all, *keep it in the fairway* and eliminate the chances of landing in the hazards by knowing your yardages, proper clubbing, shot shape, and aim.

The strategy for an approach shot on a par-4 is nearly identical to that of a par-3 of the same length, with the exception of not having your ball teed up nicely on a perfectly flat piece of turf. So the first thing to do after considering the wind is to analyze your lie, then let that decide what type of shot to hit. A nice, tight lie in the fairway will allow you the chance to spin the ball and really target that pin. A fluffy lie in the rough will create a flyer, requiring you to factor in some extra carry and roll. Hardpan or fairway bunker, if hit properly, will give you about the same amount of spin as a tight fairway lie.

Next, calculate your yardage to within a few yards, if possible, then choose a club to match the lie and distance. Make sure to know distance to the pin, as well as the front and back of the green, to eliminate any chance of missing the short stuff. Also know how far you will need to hit the ball to carry any bunkers or water protecting the green. Dial in that club, then begin your pre-shot routine.

When aiming, make sure not to go for a sucker pin, and always try to leave the ball below the hole, unless the risk of doing so is too great. Look for a nice, flat part of the green that you can safely two-putt from, and aim for it. Take a practice swing, then let it fly. Don't take too long to hit the ball, as this will allow negative thoughts to creep in. Just do it!

Playing a Par-5

The first thing to determine on a par-5 is whether or not you can realistically reach it in two. Many amateurs know inside that they cannot, but they go for the heroic second shot anyway, usually swinging too hard and flubbing it completely, insuring at least bogey. The best strategy, in my opinion, is to plan for a comfortable 70- to 100-yard lay-up shot, your best chance at making par or better. Remember that, for most of us, a par-5 hole is the best chance we have at birdie. Why waste it with aggressive heroics?

Let's take a look at two different par-5s. The first is a 468-yard dogleg left, comfortably reachable by anyone with decent length and a good fairway wood or long iron game. Generally, you have to play this hole as if it were a long par-4, hitting your drive into a part of the fairway that allows a good approach shot into the green. In order to do this, the green must be receptive to a long iron or fairway wood shot, one that will have more roll to it than a normal middle or short iron approach. If the green is small or protected in front by bunkers or water, forget about going for it in two. But if the green is soft, has some depth, and is open in front, then you might have a good chance.

Choose your landing spot in the fairway carefully. It should allow the best angle possible into the green, and also allow a decent recovery shot if your approach goes astray. This means no chips or pitches over sand or water, no deep rough, and no recovery shots to a pin that is close to the edge of the green.

Once you choose the best landing spot, simply treat the shot as you would a par-4.

If the par-5 is much longer than 470 yards or so, seriously consider laying up. Doing so will ease tension, allow you to hit a more lofted club, and increase your chances of making par or birdie. To play the long par-5, think backward from the pin. Know where the pin is located, then decide where the ideal approach wedge shot should be hit from (usually the side of the fairway opposite the side of the green with the pin). Know exactly where that nice, little 85-yard approach shot will come from, then work backward from there. To place the ball in that perfect wedge territory, you will want to hit a second shot with no more than a middle iron, for accuracy. If that means a 6-iron for you, for example (a club you might hit a reliable 160 yards), backtrack and calculate where *that* shot should be hit from. Do so by adding the wedge shot distance to the 6-iron distance— let's say about 245 yards. If the par-5 is playing 500 yards, that leaves you with a tee shot of about 255 yards, meaning driver for most of us. The big variable here will be what club you will use for your second shot; just try to make it as short a club as possible to insure a perfectly placed wedge shot into the pin.

Those of us who are shorter off the tee will most likely want to hit a lofted fairway wood for the second shot, as they are easier to hit than a long iron or 3-wood. That second shot should always be made with a club you have great confidence with, usually *not* a 3-wood or 2-iron for most of us. The name of the game is to eliminate as much risk as possible and to set up a nice short iron shot into the green.

The Art of Putting

Of all the aspects of golf, putting is, I think, the most individualized, allowing for the most variance in technique. No two Tour pros have the same putting style, yet most perform incredibly well on the greens. Pros almost always average under 1.8 putts per hole, with the top ten putters always getting close to 1.7, a figure that translates to 30 or 31 putts per round. If you watch the pros putt, you quickly learn that there is no "correct" method. What is important is being able to read the green, stroke the ball on the proper line, and get it into the hole, period. Whether it's Tom with his current cross-handed style, Ben Crenshaw with his smooth, languid, inside-out stroke, Rocco Mediate with his long putter, or Billy Mayfair with his unique cut-across stroke, what counts is consistently putting the ball into the hole.

As this book leans toward the strategic more than the instructional, I won't delve deeply into the fundamentals of putting, but rather I will present the strategies to use that will allow you the best opportunity at succeeding on the greens. There are some basic guidelines, though, that will help you be more consistent:

- Use a putter you are comfortable with. Make sure the flat stick you use is aesthetically pleasing to your eye and isn't too long or too short for your frame. You should be able to set up to the ball and grip the club on the grip, not partially on the shaft.

If you prefer a crouched-over stance (like Nicklaus), use a relatively short putter. If you like to be
in a more upright posture (like Tiger), then go
with a longer stick.

- Whatever grip you decide to use, avoid strangling the
club, which could result in jerky movement and
lots of mis-hits.

- Keep your left wrist firm through impact, and avoid
an overly "wristy" stroke, which makes distance
control more difficult.

- Try to hit the ball on the sweet spot of the club face
for the ideal feel and distance control.

- Keep your head and lower body as still as possible.
Actually, try to keep your head down even after
the ball is away. Nick Faldo suggests waiting until
you hear the ball fall into the cup before looking
up. Doing so will keep you still and solid through
the stroke.

- Set up with the ball directly below your eyes to give
yourself a proper view of the line.

- Practice, practice, practice!

Give Yourself the Best Putt Possible

Good putting starts out in the fairway. When Tom and I are
deciding on the ideal landing spot for an approach shot to a
green, we are thinking about the upcoming putt, hoping to create a birdie opportunity. That means not only getting close but

also avoiding difficult putts, such as anything downhill or a putt that has one or more severe breaks to it. All players, if given the choice, want to be left with a short, flat putt or one slightly uphill. Unlike amateurs, Tour players usually like some break to their putts, as it lends a certain predictability to the shot.

Know the green you are hitting to. Don't just be happy with landing the ball anywhere on the green; try instead to place the ball in the best spot possible, usually below the hole, leaving a nice uphill shot. Leaving yourself with a twenty-foot downhill putt is the surest way to three-putt, the scourge of amateurs and pros alike. If you could guarantee yourself a maximum of two putts per hole, your handicap would be cut by an easy four to eight strokes.

Perfecting your chipping and pitching game is another way to guarantee fewer putts per round. If your approach shot has missed the green by five to twenty yards, you must develop the ability to get that ball in close to the pin, hopefully within five feet, to save par. Also, improving your chipping and pitching skills will help improve your putting poise, as it will increase the odds of you holing a high number of short putts. By doing so, your confidence will soar.

Approaching the Green

Even before getting to the green, the pros check its overall design. As you are walking up to the green, check its slope and design from about thirty or forty yards out to get a good, full perspective. This is especially easy to do if the green lies below the fairway. Seeing it from this distance gives you the opportunity to see it in its entirety. Many greens are sloped from back to front, if only by a few inches. This type of slope change will only be apparent from a distance, so look for it.

On the Green

Once on the green, the first thing the pros do is get a full read of the putt awaiting them. They look at the line from behind, from in front, and from the side to analyze the break, the grain, and the overall condition of the grass. You should do the same, in a timely and methodical fashion. If others are to putt before you, carefully watch how their putts break and how fast they run. Be sure to notice how the balls break when very close to the hole, as this will often determine success or failure for you. As putts get closer to the hole, they slow down and are more affected by the break. Noticing the path of your opponent's ball as it decelerates will help you aim your shot properly and improve your chances of making it.

Before settling into your final read from six to ten feet behind your ball, make absolutely sure that you have prepared your ball thoroughly by properly marking it and wiping it off with a towel. Remember, any mud or grass on your ball will adversely affect its roll, increasing the odds of a miss. After doing so, make sure to carefully and completely remove any and all loose impediments along your line. Rocks, leaves, twigs, divot material, cigarette butts, or litter should all be removed without you actually stepping on your line or disturbing your ball. Then make sure to repair any ball marks that might also be in the way. Do not, of course, repair spike marks, as you will incur a penalty.

Now make your final read. Most Tour players crouch down and really give it a hard look to get a feel for the break. They also make note of the grain at this point and whether or not it will affect the speed and direction of the putt. The grain on bent grass greens has only a negligible effect on the direction of a putt, but it will still be a factor. The grain on Bermuda greens, however, is more wiry and evident and will substantially affect the course of your putt. Bermuda grass usually grows toward the setting sun, whereas bent grass toward the drainage. Poa annua, another type of greens grass common to many seasonal climactic zones, is similar to bent grass, though it can be more bumpy, which affects the line of slower putts.

If the grain of the grass on a green is growing in one direction, the ball will be slightly deflected in that general direction. If the slope of the green leans in the same direction as the grain, the putt will break more than your eye tells you it will. If the slope goes against the grain, less break will occur. If the grain points downhill, your putt will travel faster than expected; if uphill, slower. Obviously, being aware of the grain is a crucial factor.

Take a look at the green from somewhere near its middle. In one direction, the grass will appear shiny; in the other, duller and darker. Putting toward the shiny part means you are going down grain and should hit the ball slightly easier than the putt calls for; putting into the darker section means you are going into the grain and should give the ball an extra few percent of effort. The only way to confirm the effects of grain on your course is to put in enough time on the practice green, which will have the same overall qualities as the greens on the course.

Any putt that appears to be flat will probably break slightly toward any water present because the green will be engineered to drain in that direction. Also, if there is a mountain or tall hill nearby, your putt will likely break away from it.

Try to trust your first impression of the break of the putt. Don't fabricate a break if there simply is none. If it looks straight, play it that way. If you see a left-to-right break, go for it. Don't talk yourself out of your first good impression, which is usually dead on.

Some players like to read a break and then aim their putts at a spot somewhere to the side of the cup, concentrating on hitting the ball straight to that spot and ignoring the cup completely, hoping that the ball will gracefully ark into the cup. Others see the break as a whole and visualize the ball turn nicely, right into the hole. It's all a matter of personal choice, but try to stick with whatever method you choose.

Speed, or how hard you hit the ball, has a tremendous effect on the amount of break of a putt. A putt hit at one speed might break two or three inches, whereas the same putt hit at twice the speed might not break at all. Hitting it harder can eliminate a troublesome and unpredictable break, but it might result in a long comeback putt if missed. Conversely, hitting a putt too softly will create more break, also resulting in a miss. Deciding which way to go can often be a difficult decision, one that depends on the situation at hand. Generally, making an aggressive swat at the ball should only be done if you have nothing to lose and everything to gain, such as when a birdie is absolutely necessary to halve or win a hole or tournament. If the ball drops in, you have succeeded. If it misses, your six-foot comeback putt is redundant. If, however, you are leading by a shot or two, rapping the ball to reduce the break doesn't make much sense. A better tactic is to simply hit the ball with just enough force to let it die into the hole or stop within a few inches of it. Normally, you can get away with hitting an uphill putt harder than a downhill attempt, as gravity will prevent the ball from going too far past if missed.

Learning how to effectively lag putt is one of the keys to lowering your scores on the course. From what I have seen working Wednesday pro-ams with Tom, lag putting skills among amateurs leave much to be desired and are one of the main causes of high scores (and broken clubs). More than any other skill on the green, you must be able to lag a long putt to at least within three or four feet of a hole, preferably closer. Most amateurs either overcook a thirty- or forty-footer blowing it by the hole at least five or six feet, or else they chicken out and decelerate the putter, leaving the ball five or six feet short.

Learning to lag putt properly involves developing a real feel for the relationship between distance and length of putter backswing. The only way to develop this feel is to practice lots of forty-footers, over and over again, to eventually develop the instinctive muscle memory in your hands. In addition to practicing the longer putts, try putting five or six consecutive long-distance putts, each one five feet longer than the previous one. Doing so will really help ingrain the feel of lag putting and help lower your scores.

In conjunction with perfecting long-putt distance control, you must become deadly from within three to five feet. Many amateurs seem to make few of these putts, adding unnecessary strokes to their scores. So, to take advantage of your newfound lagging skills, you must be able to make those short second putts. Practice them by placing ten or twelve balls around a hole at about three to five feet away and then sinking them. Don't stop until you are able to make all of them without a miss.

A Word on the "Yips"

Aging Tour pros and amateurs alike can become afflicted with the "yips" around their mid-forties. A little-understood phenomena affecting the neuromuscular systems, players afflicted with it seem to no longer be able to make putts inside of ten feet. Hogan, Snead, Watson, Faldo, and Langer are but a few of the famous victims of this annoying problem. Some never get over it, whereas others (such as Langer and Watson) seem to work out a solution by experimenting with different putting styles, discussing the problem with neurologists and/or sports psychologists, or trying a different putter. Langer overcame his problem by switching over to a long putter, with which he now has great success.

If you find yourself missing lots of shorter putts, first go back to fundamentals. Make sure on those short putts that you are moving the putter head straight back and through, directly on the same line as the putt. Make a narrow alleyway with tees stuck in the turf and move your putter head inside of it, insuring a straight pathway. Be sure not to have any lower body movements during the putt, and do not look up until well after the ball is off and running. Also, make sure to have a firm left wrist in order to avoid any "flippyness" in the stroke.

Next, try using a different putter for a while. Often, something as simple as this can solve the problem. Try a mallet style, goose-neck, long putter, or some style different from what you are used to. Surprisingly, it can help refocus you and bring back good putting success.

Common Mistakes Made by Amateurs

As I have said before, every Wednesday before a tournament proper, the Tour players participate in a pro-am competition. Paired with the best golfers in the world, executives, celebrities, and sponsor dignitaries end up having the time of their lives and go home with a renewed respect for just how good Tour players really are.

During the round, Tom and I get to see just how much some of these amateurs struggle through the game, often sporting scores even higher than their handicaps might indicate. Though some of the problem can be attributed to nerves, much of it comes from blatant errors in strategy and equipment selection, as well as fundamental flaws in technique and execution. In this section I will attempt to touch on the most common amateur mistakes that I see out there and also attempt to offer some suggestions that might help correct them.

Bad Grip

Many amateurs adopt a grip that is too weak, meaning that the lead hand is turned so that only one or two knuckles are visible to the player's eye, with the trailing hand placed too much on top of the grip. This type of grip often results in weak shots that slice badly due to an open club face at impact. Slicing seems to be the most common shot shape of amateurs, and I believe that weak grips contribute to this. Most amateurs would be better off adopting a stronger grip, one that exposes at least three knuckles of the lead hand to the golfer's eye and reposi- tions the trailing hand to a position more underneath the grip. Tom is always strengthening the grips of pro-am partners on Wednesdays, usually with good results. This stronger grip will reduce slices by helping to square up the club head at impact. Paul Azinger, Freddie Couples, and Tiger Woods all use a strong grip and do quite well with it.

Flawed Swing

Let's face it—many of us just don't have a pretty swing. And though the look of a swing is less important than the position of the club head at impact, the fact remains that most ugly swings produce ugly impact positions, resulting in bad shots. Most of the amateurs we have played with have out-to-in swings, resulting in overly steep approach angles, poor ball contact, shanks, huge divots, and horrendous slices. Some amateurs go the other direction and have an extremely shallow, in-to-out swing that results in severe hooks and equally bad ball contact. As most of us are self-taught, having some glaring swing fault is to be expected. My answer to this is simple; go take a few lessons with a local PGA professional, who will be able to quickly put you on the right track. Often, problems that might take an amateur years to cure can be fixed in one hour by an observant pro.

Another sobering technique that can help you catch swing flaws is to have someone videotape your swing. Believe me, no matter what you think your swing looks like, it will appear significantly different to you on tape. Recording yourself in this fashion will reveal your swing path, your tempo, and a dozen other factors that could be affecting your performance.

Bad Tempo

If you watch any pro swing the club, odds are you will see a graceful, flowing, almost effortless act. Ernie Els's swing is a perfect example; dubbed the "Big Easy," there is an almost hypnotic quality to his swing, languid and relaxed, yet powerful. Fred Couples's swing is the same—flowing and easy, yet tremendously powerful. In essence, they have perfect tempo.

Most amateurs lack proper tempo in their swings, racing

through the act as if there was a half-second time limit on it. This results in decreased distance and erratic impact, two major flaws responsible for inflated handicaps.

When on the practice tee, try to remember to slow down and smooth out your swing a bit. Think tempo. Picture Ernie or Fred hypnotically flowing through the ball instead of hacking at it like it was a tree trunk. Count off "one, two" for the backswing and "three, four" for the downswing. By doing so, you will create more club head speed, hit the ball farther, and make more consistent contact, resulting in better shots and more fairways and greens in regulation. Relaxing your swing will reduce arm tension and calm you down, too, creating better overall focus and confidence.

Poor or Nonexistent Pre-shot Routine

As discussed earlier, having a repeatable pre-shot routine is an essential ingredient in every Tour player's arsenal. Unfortunately, most amateurs have an erratic or nonexistent pre-shot routine, causing them to lose focus and allow negative images to flood in. Some approach the ball, look at the target, take a few practice swings, and then let go with a swing, while others address the ball, freeze for a minute, then swing halfheartedly. To be effective, a pre-shot routine must include some form of address, aiming, waggle, and shot visualization, and it must be repeatable every time. Whatever the process you choose, the routine must function as a focusing device and must block out all negative thoughts.

Poor Alignment

As most amateurs slice, they tend to begin aiming farther and farther left in order to allow for the trajectory of the ball. Unfortunately, aiming more left tends to promote an even worse slice, as it causes an exaggerated, cutting-cross motion. Some real bananas results—weak, high shots that streak across the fairway from left to right, with the poor, brand-new ball almost always landing in an unplayable or hidden lie.

Learning proper alignment mechanics can help immensely in reducing slices, hooks, pushes, or pulls. Always put clubs down while at the practice range to help with this. Use one parallel to the path of the ball and one parallel to the plane of your feet, hips, and shoulders.

Poor Club Selection

During Wednesday pro-ams, I almost always lie to our amateur partners about their distances to the hole usually adding on about five or ten yards. When I do this, they more often put their balls on the green. This funny little trick proves to me that amateurs never quite know how far they can hit each of their clubs on a consistent basis, and they usually play for the perfect shot, which might occur only once or twice per round.

In order to correct this, make sure you are intimately familiar with the average distance you can swat each of your clubs. Take the average of ten or twelve shots and throw out the mis-hits. In doing so, you will end up hitting twice as many greens in regulation. And, when in doubt, *use one more club*. Amateurs almost always under-club themselves on shots, especially approach shots and second shots on par-5s. They remember that one perfect shot they hit with that club once and think they can repeat it again and again. Unfortunately, that rarely happens for them.

Additionally, make sure you know the exact yardage to your target. And remember, if in doubt, use more club. The trouble behind a green is almost never as bad as that in front.

Bad Equipment Selection

Many amateurs we play with don't use the right clubs. Often they use a set of irons right off the rack, even though they might have the wrong lie angles, lengths, lofts, flexes, or grip size. Some amateurs choose forged blades, which are too hard for most weekend golfers to hit.

To play effectively, you should have your set of clubs custom-fit to your body and swing. All the pros do; why shouldn't you?

Most amateurs insist on hitting their drivers on every tee shot, even when the difficulty of the hole may require a 3-wood or even an iron. Learn to choose the right club for the task at hand. Remember that accuracy, not distance, is the path to lower scores. Also, many amateurs insist on carrying 2-, 3-, and 4-irons, even though they cannot hit them with any consistency. Most amateurs would do better to replace their long irons with easier-to-hit fairway woods.

Wrong Ball Selection

The pros need to use a ball that allows them to shape their shots. This usually means a high-spin ball with a soft cover. Amateurs, in an attempt to emulate the pros, often choose a high-spin ball, which only serves to amplify whatever flaws they have. A slicer who chooses a balata ball will impart even more side spin on the shot, resulting in a horrendous slice. The same goes for a player who hooks; a soft-cover ball will hook even more. Also, soft-cover balls get cut more easily and will end up costing the high-handicapper a bundle. Additionally, these high-spin balls almost always give up distance, something most amateurs cannot afford to lose.

Most weekend players would do much better choosing a low-spin distance ball, which would help to reduce slices and hooks and add much needed distance. Many low-spin distance balls are now being made with a softer cover to aid with feel on the greens.

Improper Tee Height

Most amateurs tee up the ball too low for driver and too high for irons or fairway woods off the tee. Perhaps accustomed to using smaller-headed drivers off the tee, amateurs who purchase newer titanium drivers with huge heads fail to take into consideration the club head's increased height and often tee the ball up so that the top of the ball barely sticks up above the top of the club head. To insure better contact, higher trajectory, and longer carry, make sure to tee the ball up high enough to insure that the top of the driver head is even with the equator of the ball. With some of the huge club heads available today, that might require you to purchase extra-long tees, perhaps a two and three-quarter inch instead of the normal two and one-fourth inch.

Conversely, when hitting an iron of lofted fairway wood off the tee at a par-3 or short par-4, most amateurs tee the ball up too high, usually almost as high as for a driver. This can result in pop-ups, whiffs, or weak shots. Instead, tee the ball up just enough to mimic a nice fluffy lie, then simply hit the ball as if it were sitting in the fairway. Sweep it away with a fairway wood, or hit with a slightly descending blow with an iron.

Worn Grips

Tom changes the grips on his clubs several times each season to insure a nice, tacky feel all the time. Amateurs often leave their grips on for years, resulting in a slick, frictionless feel that decreases club control and can result in the occasional flying 7-iron. Take a lesson from the pros and have your grips changed at least once per year to insure great feel and control. Additionally, wipe your grips down with a damp towel as often as possible to keep them clean and give them a sticky feel.

Alcoholic Beverages

Many amateurs like to drink during their round and often put more than a few away at the turn. Though perfectly legal and ethical, overdrinking on the course is one of the greatest causes of poor play and bad manners. When was the last time you saw a Tour pro knocking a few down at the turn? Liquor will affect your timing, focus, and coordination and add innumerable shots to your score. Why practice on improving your game if you are just going to give all those shots back to the course in the form of three beers or a flask of hard liquor?

Lack of Food or Water

Almost every Tour player and caddie I know not only has a light breakfast before a round but also eats a few snacks during play, usually a few pieces of fruit, some granola bars, or something light and energizing. All pros also keep well hydrated on the course, drinking at least a pint or two of water during the round. Amateurs often go without any food or water and pay for it without even knowing it. Even on cool days, your body needs fuel and water when asked to walk three or four miles while concentrating and to swing a club over and over. Failing to do so will result in a loss of strength and focus and higher scores.

Make sure you eat a light breakfast an hour or so before a round, and pack a banana or some other light snack away in your bag for later on. Also, take a quart of water with you, especially if playing on a warm, sunny day. Avoid overeating at the turn, though, as this can result in sluggishness on the back 9.

Poor Short Game Skills

Simply put, amateurs do not usually have good short games, primarily due to a lopsided mentality with regard to practice. Pros spend at least half of their time hitting chips, pitches, and putts, whereas amateurs love to slam away at drivers at the local range, giving their short games little, if any, time. This almost always results in bogeys or worse. The best thing you could do to lower your scores is to always start your practice sessions with at least twenty minutes of chipping and pitching and twenty minutes of putting. Then spend as much time as you want banging balls. I guarantee that doing so will result in lower scores.

Poor Distance Control on Long Putts

One of the biggest differences between the pros and amateurs occurs on the putting surface. Tour players rarely three-putt. Three-putting, however, happens regularly to high handicappers, but needn't. If you spend time each week working on your lag putts from thirty or forty feet, you will reduce your three-putting significantly. Having a two- or three-foot comeback putt is always preferable to a seven- or eight-footer. Getting out on the practice green and working on the long putts and then on the four- or five-footers will decrease your putts per round by at least four or five strokes, guaranteed.

Poor Bunker Skills

Almost every pro I know would rather be in a bunker than in the rough because hitting out of sand is a much more controllable and predictable shot for them. Know why? Because they practice sand shots regularly. Amateurs don't and pay for it on the course, often taking two, three, or four strokes to get off the beach.

Find the closest practice bunker and work on your sand shots at least once each week. Hit out of your kid's sandbox or take your sand wedge and a few balls to the beach. Whatever it takes, being able to reliably extricate yourself from the sand will take at least several shots off your score.

Cart Use

PGA Tour pros, with few exceptions, walk the course during play. This allows them to experience the course on a very personal level. You can get a feel for subtle changes in elevation and notice slope changes in the fairway and on the green as you approach your ball. Walking also helps calm the nerves and gives you time to self-talk, a good tool used to plan your next shot.

Many amateurs opt for a cart instead of walking, or else are forced to do so. I think that's a mistake. You lose the personal connection with the land and also slip into a more rushed, unfocused mindset. Playing good golf requires a certain immersion into the course; I believe a cart reduces that and can result in higher scores. When you use a cart, you approach your ball from the side, not from directly behind, because the cart path is invariably on the edge of the fairway. This prohibits you from getting a good feel for the lay of the land; you are not able to properly survey the rest of the hole, including the green ahead. One of the best ways to read an upcoming green is from way back in the fairway, while walking up to your ball. Seeing it from this distance allows a superior perspective on its overall slope; only walking straight down the fairway to your ball will give you this intimate view. A cart often takes that away.

Physical Conditioning

More and more, the pros are becoming great physical specimens. Most of them now work out religiously and participate in some form of cardiovascular activity besides walking the course. In addition, at every tournament the players have a fitness trailer available to them for workouts and for numerous types of rehabilitation work, if needed. Many players have been able to stay in a tournament, despite injury or discomfort, because of what the staff of the fitness trailer has provided them.

Two examples of how a good physical fitness regime can help your game are the stories of Rocco Mediate and David Duval. Both players lost over thirty pounds in a year's time and committed to weightlifting regimens that dramatically improved their games. Rocco also performed lots of back-strengthening exercises to overcome the effects of back surgery some years before, allowing him to finally post a well-deserved win in early 1999.

The amateurs Tom and I have played with over the years have often been overweight, stiff, and aerobically unfit, resulting in flawed mechanics and higher scores. An easy way to pick up a few strokes on each round is to simply stay in shape and do some strengthening exercises such as weight training or calisthenics. Also, try to find the time to walk, jog, swim, or ride a bike each day, and stretch out regularly to insure proper flexibility, a vital part of a successful swing. Keeping in good shape will also prevent the occurrence of injuries, especially in the aging golfer, whose game can suffer tremendously because of inflexibility and loss of strength.

Ignorance of the Weather

Tour players always pay close attention to the weather during each tournament because they know how seriously it can affect play. Strong winds or a pelting rainstorm can wreak havoc on scores; the pros need to adjust their games accordingly to remain in the hunt.

Most amateurs do not take the effects of the weather as seriously as they should. They certainly will protect their bodies and equipment from the cold, the wet, and the wind but will rarely adjust their games properly.

Most amateurs could lower their scores by learning how to

play under less than favorable conditions. Learning a good knockdown shot for the wind is one way to avoid disaster. Keeping a few balls in your pocket on a cold day is another; this will keep them warm and allow them to play longer and softer than if allowed to cool down to the outside temperature. During a cold day, Tom and I simply use a new ball on every hole, one that has been warmed inside my pocket.

Learning to play on a wet course is another necessary skill that many amateurs do not possess. Generally, if playing on soaked turf, you need to move the ball slightly back in your stance to insure contact with the ball first. Because the turf is soaked, any shot hit at all fat will be an absolute disaster. This isn't always the case on a dry course, which might allow the club head to bounce into the ball on a slightly fat shot. Just play it as if you were hitting off of hardpan; try to get just ball and no divot.

Not Playing Your Game

Often, a Tour player will come to a hole that is set up opposite to his or her strengths. For example, during Nicklaus's early career, he didn't have the ability to draw the ball very effectively; this gave him problems on dogleg-left holes. His powerful, long fades would often fly right through the hole's elbow, into rough or worse. It wasn't until the mid- to late-sixties that he finally mastered a repeatable draw that he could rely on.

Tour players, who rely on a fade or a draw only, often must play a course within their strengths and forget about trying to hit a shot that does not come easily to them. A natural drawer of the ball like Tom Lehman might not be able to pull off a high fade when needed, instead pulling the ball left into trouble. Instead, he must hit his natural draw and try to make the shot fit into the hole's design, regardless of which shot shape is called for. This might require him to hit less club to insure the ball does not carry or roll through the elbow of the dogleg-right fairway.

Amateurs should play to their strengths on the course and leave swing change exercises to the practice tee. Unfortunately I see many weekend players trying to hit shots that they do not possess, simply because the hole they are on demands it of them. This is a recipe for disaster. They get seduced and suckered by the course designer and end up with bogey or worse.

When you are on the course, only use the shots you are comfortable with. If you fade the ball, use the fade. Don't attempt to draw the ball, as this might end up putting you in out-of-bounds, rough, or trees. Conversely, if your natural shot shape is a draw, don't attempt a fade, as this might result in the same fate. If you normally hit the ball low, don't attempt to hit a high shot just because the green is small and fast or protected up front. Instead, lay up eighty or so yards away, then hit wedge. Likewise, if you always hit the ball high, do not suddenly attempt a low shot just because the wind is howling or you need to use a bump-and-run. Stick with the high shot, and play the wind as best you can.

This doesn't mean that you shouldn't ever try to change your shot shape. It just means that changes should be accomplished on the practice tee. Once you have mastered a different type of shot on the range, then you can incorporate it into your game.

Not Understanding the Lie

Every Tour player could write a book just on lie analysis. They develop an innate understanding of how the lie of the ball will dictate the type of shot needed. Amateurs rarely do so, though. Instead, they simply set up to the ball and just hack away, oblivious to the special situations that might be present.

In order to be more successful through the green, you must become a student of the lie. Know what shots are needed from the fairway, the rough, hardpan, sand, high grass, cart paths, dirt, and even water. Know what adjustments need to be made in your set-up and swing. In doing so, you will insure more pars and less frustration. Practice hitting balls from random lies; throw your practice balls down randomly and hit them from wherever they land, regardless of the lie. Master all manner of shots before using them on the course, then go out there and use them with confidence!

General Lack of Strategy

Every pro player studies a course before competing on it and develops a unique strategy or game plan before entering the "field of battle." Unfortunately, most average players simply step up to the first tee and whack away without any game plan at all. Certainly this is a recipe for bogey golf.

Know the course and develop a specific game plan for defeating it. Study the yardage book, know yardages, memorize where trouble is, and know what shot is needed for each situation. Know the angles and best percentage shots from each location on the course. Make golf an artful science instead of a frustrating way to kill five hours of time.

Trying the Miracle Shot

Many amateurs get themselves into trouble, then try to pull off an impossibly heroic shot to get out of jail. All they end up doing is digging themselves a deeper grave. Even pros, when faced with a nearly impossible shot, will take their medicine and chip or pitch back out to the fairway, unless a championship is on the line and they have nothing to lose. They will accept bogey and move on, knowing that a sure bogey is better than a possible double or triple. I have seen amateurs opt for impossible full-swing recovery shots simply because the chipping and pitching parts of their games were so poor that they doubted their abilities to get back into the fairway.

When you get into a situation that provides you with only a slim chance for pulling off that heroic shot, take your medicine and just get the ball back into the fairway. The exception to this, though, would be if you were playing a laid-back practice round, taking two or more shots each time, wanting to experiment and practice unusual recovery shots. If this is the case, and you are not even keeping score, then by all means try threading the ball through that grove of trees, or smashing it out of that waist-high hay field.

Poor Mental Outlook

No Tour pro ever wins a tournament solely based on his or her physical talents. He or she must combine those skills with the proper mental outlook in order to win. That is why, on any given day, an unknown player can beat the best in the world. He or she had more confidence and a more positive outlook, or else simply had less on his or her mind at the time. A winner can block out all else going on and concentrate on the game. Ben Hogan was famous for never knowing the scores of his playing partners because he focused so intently on the task at hand.

You should be the same way. Go into your round with an air of calm indifference about you. Be positive and determined. Rely on a good pre-shot routine to clear your mind of negative thoughts, and then just swing away. Visualize your shots going exactly where you want them to. Never think too hard about where you *don't* want your ball to go; instead, think about where you *do* want it to go, and let it happen. And think less about playing your opponent and more about playing the course. The good score that ensues will take care of that little Nassau bet you have going on the side.

Try to curb your anger on the course. Wrath and self-deprecation will only serve to destroy your concentration and confidence. If you hit a poor shot, think about what went wrong, then let it pass and focus on the next shot. Let the round become a series of challenges instead of one overwhelming task. You know the old Confucian saying: "A journey of a thousand miles begins with one step." Corny, but true. A round of golf should be seventy, eighty, ninety or one hundred individual shot challenges pieced together into one fulfilling event, instead of four hours of aggravation.

Do not panic if you have made a terrible score on one hole. You can always redeem yourself on the next. Do not let those evil golf demons defeat you! Just let go of the frustration and have fun. If you find yourself about ready to hit your eighth or ninth shot on a horrific hole, consider simply picking up your ball and moving on to the next tee. Putting an end to a nightmarish hole in this way can often help flush out the agony. Just give in to the fact that the course beat you for that moment and move on. Be positive, yet humble, when the course defeats you.

Try not to have too many swing thoughts in your head while on the course. The pros strive to free themselves of this confusing trap while competing, as it prevents them from concentrating on strategy. You should save the mechanical thoughts for the practice range to keep your mind free and clear while playing a round. The most mechanical thought Tom ever has in his head while competing might be "take it back slow" or "full follow-through." He saves the mechanical minutiae for the range. You should do the same; do not go through a ten-point checklist before each shot. It will only serve to short-circuit your brain.

Most of all, can the negative thoughts. Most amateurs we play with talk negatively about an upcoming shot, saying things like "I always hit it into the water here" or "I hate this hole." Believe me, doing so is the kiss of death. Tour pros and caddies never verbalize negative thoughts, as they will seep in and destroy any hope of victory. Remember, *think positive*. Brim with confidence. In doing so, you will program your mind for success.

How the Pros Prepare and Practice

All Tour pros put in some amount of practice and preparatory time on a regular basis in order to maintain their games, work out niggling problems, and get ready for a particular course coming up in the rotation. Just how much time they spend on these three things can vary tremendously, according to the individual. Tom tends to spend a great amount of time practicing, whereas a player such as Mark Calcavecchia puts in much less time. It's all up to the individual and where his or her game is at the time. As always, in golf you do what works for you.

The question of maintenance is an especially subjective one; some players can get away with minimal time on the range, whereas others have to close the place down. A player like Ben Hogan, for instance, literally practiced until his hands bled because he felt he needed to. Other pros might put in only a few minutes during an off day, and even a minimal period of time before and after a competitive round, because they feel their games are up to par and need no further tweaking. The best golfers, however, tend to spend more time preparing and practicing than do others. Nicklaus, for example, would always come to Augusta a week before the Masters and play numerous practice rounds there just to get his game dialed in to the unique conditions, particularly the lightning-fast greens and the lack of substantial rough. In comparison, most players do not pull in to Augusta until the Monday or Tuesday before the championship.

The Tour player has nearly impeccable skills in comparison to the average golfer. Because of this, there is much less of a need to actually improve his or her overall game and more of a desire to "troubleshoot" or pick up on any irregularities that might pop up, such as a slight swing plane change or an improper hip clearance. Most, however, will always work hard on maintaining a solid, repeatable stance as well as proper alignment to the target. If you watch Tom on the practice range, he will invariably have several clubs down on the grass, aiding him in his set-up and alignment. In fact, one reason the pros might be the best in the world is their devotion to maintaining perfect fundamentals, including grip, alignment, set-up, and pre-shot routine.

The average golfer should think about improvement rather than maintenance. For instance, if you are currently a 20 handicapper, do you have any desire at all to *maintain* that level of skill, or do you want to cut strokes? Accordingly, you need to spend more time on the range and the practice green, working on making consistent contact and learning how to master an arsenal of necessary shots, from the basic bunker shot or a soft draw to the 40-yard wedge shot or the 60-foot lag putt. Once a shot is mastered (if there ever is such a thing), you can then work it just enough to keep it sharp. As a matter of fact, most pros stop practicing a particular shot once they have hit it perfectly a few times. This is done for a very good reason; when you end an activity on a positive note, that upbeat feeling tends to be ingrained in your memory and easily recalled when needed. Conversely, if you end your practice on a bad note (say, a topped 5-iron), your mind will store that feeling and draw on it the next time you have to hit that club. The moral here is to work on something until you have done it right a few times, then stop.

Not even a Tour pro can hit a golf ball consistently, day in and day out, without having some kind of niggling little (or not so little) problem creep in. When this occurs, he or she usually spends downtime between tournaments or off-season time working on fixing what's wrong. For many of the pros, this involves working with a professional teacher, such as Butch Harmon or David Leadbetter, whose job it is to spot the problem and invent a cure. For instance, Vijay Singh had for too long a time a major problem with his putting, falling far down in the Tour putting statistics. Then, a short time before the 1998 PGA Championship, Vijay switched to a "left hand-low" putting grip in an attempt to stabilize his stroke and keep his left hand from breaking down. The results of this switch were better than he could have hoped for, winning the tournament and vastly improving his overall putting statistics. By concentrating on fixing his faltering putting, he allowed the rest of his stellar game to shine through.

If you can easily identify a problem you are having, try to concentrate more of your practice time on eliminating that problem. A slice, for instance, the bane of so many golfers, can ruin a person's round. Just as many of the pros now do, you should consult with a local PGA pro for advice on how to eliminate the problem instead of second-guessing or taking advice from other high-handicappers. A well-timed lesson or two can save you from years of bad play. Why not spend the money on a qualified teacher instead of another "miracle" driver?

Most pros try to fine-tune practice sessions to an upcoming tournament. For example, Augusta National has lots of holes that require a right-to-left movement on the ball. Because of this, players will often practice hitting more draws than fades beforehand. At the annual Doral-Ryder Tournament in Florida, the famed "blue monster" course has what seems like a thousand bunkers, causing players to bone up on all of their bunker shots. Before playing in the British Open, virtually all the players work hard on hitting low, boring, wind-cheating shots to deal with the ever-present breezes that blow there. Whatever the course, there will be a particular type of shot or shots that will need to be used, causing the pros to practice it beforehand.

You should do the same. If you know you will be playing on a particularly windy course, for example, make sure to practice hitting low knockdown shots before your round. Or if the course has fast greens, make sure to become familiar with the speed of the practice green before venturing out on the course. In order to know what to expect from a course you have never played before, consider asking the club pro for some basic insights and try to obtain a yardage book, which will at least show you what to expect in terms of length, hole shape, and location of hazards.

When Tom Kite goes to the practice range, he goes with a plan, unlike most amateurs, who hit buckets of balls without having a clear goal in mind. Tom may just want to loosen up, work on a special shot, or diagnose a swing glitch. Often I have stood behind him and, at his request, watched the plane of his swing, his footwork, or whether the club head is open or closed at the top. These are factors that need to be discovered and modified on the practice tee, not during a round.

Just as you need a clear, concise strategy on the course, so do you need a strategy on the practice range. You cannot just go and pound balls with your driver all day and think that it will improve your game. If anything, that kind of thoughtless golf will hurt your scores and your ability to focus.

Amateurs normally say they are going to the driving range; pros say they are going to the *practice* range. This interesting fact points out one of the most glaring mental errors amateurs make. You should never blindly bang away with your big stick before first warming up with your short irons. Before a round, Tom always starts out with easy pitch shots with a wedge, then slowly works up to full shots with the short irons. Only after he is totally loose and stretched out does he move up to the longer clubs, with which he will hit far fewer shots than with the shorter clubs, the scoring irons. If Tom hits a few great drives, he will put that club down and go back to hitting wedge shots.

Always finish your practice or warm-up with some short wedge shots to establish good rhythm and tempo. Try to nail a target with the ball. Develop a real feel with your wedges. Without it, you will never make a birdie and will be hard-pressed to pull off par half the time. The wedge must be as deadly a club in your hands as the putter or driver. The pros know that, and so should you. Often, Tom will put in a special practice session just with his "finesse," or lob wedge. I will pace off and mark every ten-yard increment, and then he will attempt to hit this scoring wedge right to each marker. In this way, he ingrains the feel for thirty-, forty-, fifty-, sixty- and seventy-yard shots, so vital to making birdies. Try this exercise; you won't regret it.

When a trip to the range is not a warm-up for a round, you should go with a definite plan. Say, for instance, you've been having trouble hitting your 5-iron flush and want to rectify the problem. Instead of taking all of your clubs to the range, why not just bring the 5-iron and perhaps a pitching wedge to warm up with? After hitting a dozen or so easy wedge shots, begin hitting the 5-iron, at first taking easy swings, then working up to a full swing, always aiming at a precise target. The object here is to get a feel for what the problem might be and then experiment enough to solve the dilemma. Once you have hit a number of good, clean shots, though, stop right there. Remember always to quit on a positive note so that the feeling of success, not failure, stays with you.

When on the practice tee, don't just hit the same type of shot with each club. For instance, after hitting a normal 8-iron, try hitting a knockdown 8. Then hit a hard cut with it, and then a high draw. Try to hit a driver half your normal distance. Bump-and-run a 5-iron, or see if you can hit a laid-open 6-iron as high as a normal 9-iron. Hit a straight shot by drawing a 3-wood into a strong left-to-right wind. Being creative and developing feel in these ways will make you a much better golfer.

While on the range, try your hand at shot imagery, seeing the shot occur before you actually hit it. The Tour pros do this all the time, as it helps prepare the mind and body to pull off the real thing. See your drive gently fade right to the spot you chose as the target. Imagine your wedge shot arcing high up and coming down right in front of the one hundred-yard sign. Believe me, it really works.

While on the range, don't forget to work on the essentials, such as alignment, ball position, grip, and pre-shot routine. Tom always puts a few clubs down on the range to help him with alignment. If he finds the need, so should you.

The practice frame of mind should differ somewhat from the competitive frame of mind. When on the range or playing a practice round, Tom and other Tour players still work somewhat on mechanics, making sure their swings are grooved, their tempos smooth, and their set-up positions sound. During a practice round, Tom will often hit more than one approach shot from any given position just to see how different parts of each green hold the shot, or to attack potential pin placements. For instance, he may hit a ball to the back of a back-to-front sloped green just to see how well the green holds a long iron shot. Then he may hit from the same position to another part of the green to see if that might be the better percentage shot. If you are out playing a round alone or with a good friend, with no one behind you, consider hitting two or three shots just to get a feel for how different parts of the green are accepting the ball.

While playing a practice round, Tom and I are basically relearning the course at hand. We want to renew our knowledge of yardages, conditions, slope and grain of greens, best landing zones on each fairway, and hole shapes. In addition, we want to remember where the best places to miss a shot are on each green. For example, Tom might have a 145-yard 8-iron into a pin located in the far-right portion of a relatively wide green. Normally calling for a fade, Tom will aim for the center of the green and let the ball work into the pin. This strategy is strategically more sound than attempting to hit the ball straight at the pin for an important reason. If the straight shot veers right at all, the ball will miss the green. But if the faded shot does not move right, it will still land on the green because it was initially aimed at the center. So though the shot "missed" its intended target (the pin), the ball still lands on the green. All the pros, when considering an approach shot, always plan the shot in this way. When on the range, you should practice this type of strategy. Know where to miss it on each hole. Play the same game that so many pros do; imagine that there is a tight fairway out there instead of a wide-open range. Choose a target on the right or left portion of your "fairway," then hit a fade or draw right to it. If the ball doesn't move as much as you wanted it to, it will still land in your imaginary fairway.

Sometimes Tom brings a video camera to the range to tape his swing in hope of catching a potential flaw in the making. You can do this, too; have a friend tape your swing, or put the camera on a tripod and tape yourself going through your bag. At first, it can be sobering to see yourself making movements you never thought you were making. Once you get over that, though, the tape will be of tremendous help in solving basic swing flaws.

All the Tour players put in at least as much time chipping, pitching, and putting as they do hitting full shots. That is what makes them so much better than all the amateurs out there. If there is one thing Tom and I consistently see wrong with an amateur partner's game on a Wednesday, it is invariably his or her short game, which is nearly always abominable. Always spend at least half your time hitting shots inside of thirty yards, perfecting tricky pitches and chips, and, above all, putting. Of all the things you can do to lower your score, short game work is the most vital.

When Tom practices before a competitive round, he gives himself plenty of time, normally getting to the practice range at least one hour before tee-off. You should emulate this habit. A slow, proper warm-up followed by some chipping, pitching, and putting will give you the upper hand on your playing partners, who often take a few swings with the driver and then hammer away. A proper warm-up will relax and loosen up your muscles, and it will provide you with the proper feel for the round ahead.

If you don't have the time to hit balls before a round, try hitting a few chips and pitches, as they will allow you to develop a sense of rhythm and tempo, so important to a successful round.

epilogue

Over the past twenty-five years, I have had a wonderful career caddying for the world's best and belonging to a select group of golf professionals lucky enough to derive a living from the best game ever. As a PGA Tour caddie, I've had access to the world's premiere courses and made lasting friendships with the finest players the world has ever known. Being part of a winning tradition with Tom Kite has been both an honor and a privilege; thanks, boss, for giving me the opportunity to add a footnote or two to the pages of golfing history.

I decided to write this book in order to pass along to you years of golfing experience, culled from the countless fairways walked, yardages reckoned, clubs pulled, and victories shared. Hopefully I have accomplished this and opened a few windows for you onto life on Tour.

From the early rounds I caddied as a boy to the 1992 U.S. Open victory at Pebble Beach, I have enjoyed every moment. I am proud of what I have accomplished as a caddie on Tour, and I know that my efforts have in some small way contributed to Tom's fabulous success. Trying to move beyond that, this book has attempted to put me, a professional Tour caddie, on your bag in an effort to lower your scores and make the game more enjoyable and meaningful.

The game of golf has never been more popular and exciting than it is right now. With great young stars like Tiger Woods, David Duval, Se Ri Pak, and Annika Sorenstam tearing up the turf, I know we will have many years of thrilling golf ahead. Combine that with the new international tournaments penciled into the PGA Tour schedule, and the entry of Tom Kite, Tom Watson, and Lanny Wadkins onto the Senior Tour, and we have got a full plate coming our way.

It is good to see so many new golfers taking up the sport, particularly the youngsters. With so many local, state, and federal municipalities introducing programs aimed at providing instruction and tee times to low-income youth, the game should enjoy an unparalleled period of growth in the next twenty years.

I believe one issue that both public and private gold officials should focus on is the reestablishment of caddie programs for youth, in an attempt to encourage involvement early on. There is no better way, in my opinion, to teach a young person about the intricacies of the game, and of life as well. Walking those fairways as an adolescent taught me to love, respect, and understand the game. Reinstituting adolescent caddie pools at as many courses and country clubs as possible will do more to popularize and democratize the game than any federal program ever could, however well meaning or well funded.

I hope this book has brought to you fresh, behind-the-scenes insights on all aspects of professional golf. Caddies are blessed with a unique perspective on the game, one that allows them to be close to all that defines golfing greatness. As one of caddying's "elder statesmen," I am happy to have provided you with this close-up view of life as a caddie and of life on Tour, as well as with an intimate look at the techniques and strategies that make PGA Tour pros the best golfers in the world. It is my fondest hope that, after reading *Caddie Sense*, you will be able to improve your skills and increase your love for the greatest of games—golf.